JUNIOR STEPS IN RE YEAR 5 TEACHER'S RESOURCE BOOK

MICHAEL KEENE

JAN KEENE

STANLEY THORNES (PUBLISHERS) LTD

Text © Michael Keene and Jan Keene 1997

The right of Michael and Jan Keene to be identified as authors of this work has been asserted by them in accordance with the Copyright, Designs and Patents Act 1988.

All rights reserved. The copyright holders authorise ONLY users of *Junior Steps in RE Year 5* to make photocopies or stencil duplicates of the Copymasters for their own or their classes' immediate use within the teaching context. No other rights are granted without permission in writing from the publisher or under licence from the Copyright Licensing Agency Limited. Further details of such licences (for reprographic reproduction) may be obtained from the Copyright Licensing Agency Limited, of 90 Tottenham Court Road, London W1P 0LP. Copy by any other means or for any other purpose is strictly prohibited without the prior written consent of the copyright holders. Applications for such permission should be addressed to the publishers.

First published in 1997 by
Stanley Thornes (Publishers) Ltd
Ellenborough House
Wellington Street
CHELTENHAM
GL50 1YW

99 00 / 10 9 8 7 6 5 4

A catalogue record for this book is available from the British Library.

ISBN 0 7487 2123 1

Typeset by Tech Set Limited, Gateshead, Tyne and Wear
Printed in Great Britain by Ashford Colour Press, Gosport, Hampshire.

CONTENTS

INTRODUCTION	V
COPYMASTER MATRIX	VIII

CHAPTER ONE: CHRISTIANITY — 1

One Church – many churches	1
The Anglican Church	3
The Roman Catholic Church	6
The Methodist Church	8
The Salvation Army	10
The Orthodox Church	13
Confirmation	15
Adult baptism	18
Marriage	20
Death	22

CHAPTER TWO: JUDAISM — 24

The Ten Sayings	24
Around birth	27
Barmitzvah and batmitzvah	29
Rosh Hashanah and Yom Kippur	31
Marriage	33
Death	35
Mourning	37

CHAPTER THREE: ISLAM — 39

Around birth	39
Family life	42
Women	44
Marriage	46
Death	48

CHAPTER FOUR: SIKHISM — 50

Name-giving	50
Serving others	55
Sharing with others	57
Wearing the turban	59
The Amrit ceremony	61
Marriage	63
Death	65

PUPILS' GLOSSARY	67
TEACHER'S GLOSSARY	72

INTRODUCTION

The terms BCE (Before Common Era) and CE (Common Era) are used throughout this series of books. They replace the more familiar BC and AD although, in practice, they mean exactly the same. This will need to be explained to the children. The new terms are more acceptable to adherents of non-Christian religions.

The words in the Pupils' Books which are in bold are included in the Keywords section at the end of each book. The same words appear in the Pupils' Glossary at the end of the Teacher's Book. The words in bold in the Teacher's Book are explained in the Teacher's Glossary.

THE EDUCATION REFORM ACT, 1988

The Education Reform Act of 1988 laid down the legal requirements for any programme of Religious Education. It stipulated that every programme should: '...reflect the fact that the religious traditions of Great Britain are, in the main, Christian whilst taking into account the other principal religions represented in Great Britain.'

This basic principle has determined the content and approach of this series of books. The Christian religion is predominant whilst considerable material on Judaism, Islam and Sikhism is also included.

THE AIMS OF RELIGIOUS EDUCATION

The Consultative Document for Religious Education, published in 1994, laid down several clear aims for the teaching of the subject at all levels. These aims stipulated that pupils should:

a) Acquire a growing knowledge and understanding of the Christian religion. They should also come by a close understanding of the other main religions which have a strong following in Great Britain. In practice this is likely to involve a study of Judaism, Islam, Sikhism, Hinduism and Buddhism. At Key Stage 2, however, pupils are only required to study Christianity and two other religions.
b) Develop some understanding of the influence that religious beliefs and values have had, and continue to have, upon individuals and societies.
c) Develop the ability to make 'reasoned and informed judgements' about religious and moral issues. To help them to do so at Key Stage 2 this series introduces children to the teachings of four religions – Christianity, Judaism, Islam and Sikhism.
d) Have the opportunity to enhance their own 'spiritual, moral, cultural and social development' through Religious Education. This can happen in three separate, and distinct, ways:
   i) Through a growing awareness of the basic issues of life and death – and their links with religious teachings.
   ii) Through a response to these basic issues in the light of the children's own personal experiences.
   iii) Through a reflection on personally held beliefs, values and experiences.
e) Develop a positive attitude towards other people – especially those who hold different beliefs and opinions to their own. A fundamental purpose of Religious Education is the inculcation of a greater tolerance towards others through knowledge and understanding.

THE CORE OF A SYLLABUS

Agreed Syllabuses are determined locally. The new Model Syllabuses are not legally binding. They will, however, form the basis of any Agreed Syllabus drawn up in the foreseeable future. The Consultation Document insists that all Agreed Syllabuses should contain a core which:

a) Reflects the religious situation in Great Britain. Although Britain has become a multiracial society since the 1950s it is still historically, and practically, very much a Christian society.

All documents refrain from stipulating just what percentage of the Religious Education syllabus should be Christian. After all, the word 'predominant' can mean no more than 51%. In *Junior Steps in RE* it has been assumed that the Christian content of the overall syllabus will be between 55% and 60%.

b) Takes into account the other religious traditions which now have a firm place in British society.
c) Ensures that all children between the ages of 15 and 18 have the opportunity of acquiring 'a coherent knowledge and understanding of all the principal religious traditions represented in Great Britain.'
d) Provides an opportunity for every child to develop spiritually, morally, culturally and religiously. Within this overall framework it is envisaged that the Agreed Syllabuses will give as much local freedom as possible to teachers.

THE TWO MODEL SYLLABUSES

The Model Syllabuses, first published in 1994, are not statutory documents. They are intended to be used by Conferences drawing up Locally Agreed Syllabuses. It is expected, however, that they will undergird the teaching of Religious Education in schools at all levels.

Two 'Models' were provided. They are:

A) Model One. A structure which is based on a knowledge and understanding of what it means to be a member of a faith community.
B) Model Two. A structure which emphasises the main beliefs of the different religious communities.

In practice, any coherent programme of Religious Education within a school will need to take both of these aspects into account. Practice and belief cannot be separated. One inevitably springs from and leads to the other. The two will be constantly intertwined in *Junior Steps in RE*.

AIMS (ACHIEVEMENT TARGETS) APPLIED TO KEY STAGE 2

By the time they have completed Key Stage 2 all pupils should have had the opportunity to:

1. **Learn about religion.** They should have acquired a developing knowledge of Christianity and two other religions by:
   - coming into contact with important religious objects and artefacts, places and people.
   - exploring some of the important activities (e.g. worship, singing, prayer, etc.) connected with the different religions.
   - seeing that some features (e.g. festivals, worship, etc.) have common ingredients in more than one religion – although they might be expressed rather differently from one religious community to another.
   - studying some of the people who are held up in the different faith communities as examples.
   - looking at the meanings of symbols and stories within the different communities.
   - beginning to appreciate, and understand, the different beliefs of the various religions.

   The pupils should be encouraged to look for the signs of the impact of religion on the society around them and in the lives of individual believers.

2. **Learn from religion.** According to the Model Syllabuses this should take place in three ways:
   a) As a response by pupils to religious and moral issues by:
      - considering the usefulness of religious practices – such as prayer and meditation – in their own lives.
      - looking at stories and religious teaching on important questions.
      - taking what is given in Religious Education and relating it to other areas of life.
   b) Taking one's own personal and spiritual development forward by:
      - discussing those matters which arise from one's own personal development.
      - showing care in listening to the opinions and beliefs of others.
      - exploring questions which relate to the meaning of life.

- developing an understanding of what it means to belong to a religious community.
- using art, music or drama to express one's deepest thoughts and feelings.
- exploring the use of space and silence.
- developing ideas of fairness.

c) Developing positive attitudes towards other people and their right to hold different points of view by:
- developing the confidence to state, and explain, one's own point of view.
- exploring religious perspectives and those areas of life with which religion is particularly involved.
- learning from the different perspectives and teachings of religious traditions.
- respecting the opinions and ideas of those who differ from us.
- showing a readiness to learn from those who think differently.
- exploring and experiencing a sense of awe and wonder.

COPYMASTER MATRIX

THEME	TITLE	COPYMASTER DESCRIPTION
CHRISTIANITY		
One Church – many churches	1. Inside a church	Label objects and answer questions on objects found in church.
The Anglican Church	2. Match up in a church	Match up definitions.
	3. What you will find in a church	Colour and cut out drawings. Paste in right place on drawing of church.
The Roman Catholic Church	4. In a Roman Catholic church	Find out the names of objects in a Roman Catholic church.
The Methodist Church	5. John Wesley and the early Methodists	Describe what is happening in the drawings and draw own picture.
The Salvation Army	6. The Salvation Army officer	Write three sentences about the life of a Salvation Army officer.
	7. The work of a Salvation Army officer	Drawing pictures and writing about people helped by the Salvation Army.
The Orthodox Church	8. The iconostasis	Draw icons on iconostasis from those shown. Colour priest and altar.
Confirmation	9. Being confirmed	Answer questions on copymaster.
	10. The Confirmation service	Cut out, colour and paste drawings of Confirmation service. Write about drawings.
Adult baptism	11. Adult baptism – what is happening?	Answer questions on sheet. Colour drawings. Write about drawings.
Marriage	12. A Christian wedding	Match up drawings with comments on sheet.
Death	13. The 23rd Psalm	Drawings to go with phrases from psalm. Explain why psalm is used at many funerals.
JUDAISM		
The Ten Sayings	14. Receiving the Ten Sayings	Paste drawings into book and write about them.
	15. The Ten Sayings	Copy Sayings and answer questions.
Around birth	16. Around birth	Answer questions on copymaster.
Barmitzvah and batmitzvah	17. The barmitzvah	Identify and describe the Torah, yad, tallit, and yarmulka. Write a sentence about each.
Rosh Hashanah and Yom Kippur	18. Blowing the shofar	Describe different sounds made by shofar and explain the significance of them.
Marriage	19. A Jewish wedding	Identify, copy and explain drawings.
Death	20. Death in a Jewish family	Match drawings with captions, write some captions.
Mourning	21. Mourning	Draw four aspects of Jewish mourning. Describe drawings.
ISLAM		
Around birth	22. What is happening?	Explain what is happening.
	23. The Adhan	Answer questions on copymaster.
Family life	24. Different families	Draw pictures of Western and Muslim families. List differences between two families.
Women	25. Women in Islam	Answer questions
Marriage	26. Choosing someone to marry	Fill in form. Discuss details with class.
Death	27. Facing up to death	Answer questions about Muslim approach to death.
SIKHISM		
Name-giving	28. Names	Find out if each name has a meaning. List six favourite names. Choose own name.
	29. Name graph	Survey to discover most popular names in class. Name grid. Answer questions on sheet.
	30. The Sikh name-giving ceremony	Describe what is happening. Draw one aspect of ceremony not illustrated.
Serving others	31. Helping other people	Write under drawings what person is doing to help others.
Sharing with others	32. Sharing in a gurdwara	Put jobs in gurdwara in right order. Draw oneself doing a job in gurdwara.
Wearing the turban	33. Tying a turban	Cut out drawings. Paste in order. Line up descriptions with drawings.
The Amrit ceremony	34. The Sikh Amrit ceremony	Explain what is happening in each drawing.
Marriage	35. A Sikh wedding	Paste drawings in order. Write two sentences about each drawing.
Death	36. A Sikh funeral	Identify four objects drawn. Write one sentence about each.

AIMS	TEACHING POINTS
To introduce features of a church building.	Different denominations within the Church; the church 'family'; points the denominations have in common.
To introduce the Anglican Church	The Church of England; font; altar; service of Holy Communion.
To introduce the Roman Catholic Church	The Roman Catholic Church; St Peter; the Pope; Mass.
To introduce the Methodist Church	John Wesley; birth of Methodist Church; hymn singing.
To introduce the Salvation Army	The Salvation Army; work of Salvation Army; Salvation Army worship; the citadel.
To introduce the Orthodox Church	The Orthodox Church; icons.
To show that Confirmation is an important service in many Christian Churches.	Confirmation; link with infant baptism; role of the bishop; laying on of hands; Holy Spirit.
To link adult baptism with Baptist Church. To show reasons for adult baptism.	Adult baptism and infant baptism; other names for adult baptism; link with Jesus; stages of adult baptism.
To show marriage as a gift from God.	Marriage as a gift from God; marriage as eternal; the ring as a symbol of eternal love; link with Jesus.
To introduce death and the Christian response to it.	Survival of the soul; purgatory and heaven; extreme unction.
To introduce the Ten Sayings as given to Moses.	The Ten Sayings; the Torah; Moses as the law-giver of Israel.
To discover how Jews welcome a new baby into their community.	Welcome given to girl and name-announcing; circumcision; Abraham.
To show the important part played by barmitzvah and, to a lesser extent, batmitzvah.	Barmitzvah, batmitzvah; the Sunday School; the reading of the Torah.
To introduce the Jewish festivals of Rosh Hashanah and Yom Kippur	Rosh Hashanah and Yom Kippur; heart-searching; the shofar.
To see the central place that marriage occupies within the Jewish community.	Marriage and the Jewish community; the Jewish wedding service; distinctive elements within this service.
To show how Jews approach death. To show how Jews deal with death.	Death and prayer; feelings of grief; Chevra Kadisha; burial.
To explain the meaning of 'mourning' and the way that it is dealt with in the Jewish community.	Mourning; return to normal life; the role of the community in helping those who grieve.
To explain what takes place in a Muslim family after a baby is born.	The Adhan; the Bismillah; the Muslim concern for the poor.
To show the nature of Muslim family life.	The importance of the family; the role of the mother; children; parents; grandparents.
To show the demands made on women in Muslim society.	The role played by women; the rules laid down by the Qur'an over dress; the role of women in worship.
To show what is distinctive about the Muslim approach to marriage.	Arranged marriages; the marriage contract; marriage ceremony; the dowry; celebrations.
To explain the Muslim approach to death.	The importance of the Adhan; equality of all after death; body facing Makkah.
To introduce the Sikh name-giving ceremony	Role of Guru Granth Sahib; drinking of amrit; eating of karah parshad.
The importance within Sikhism of service to others.	Sewa; the story of Bhal Khanaya.
The importance within Sikhism of sharing with others.	The langar; sharing with others; the meal in the langar; the examples of Guru Nanak and Guru Amar Das.
To introduce the meaning that long hair has for a Sikh.	The importance of long hair and tidiness; children and their hair; the turban.
To introduce the Amrit ceremony and link it with the Khalsa.	Amrit ceremony; the Khalsa; background to the Khalsa; importance of amrit; rules of the Khalsa.
To introduce the Sikh marriage ceremony.	Anand Karaj; importance of Guru Granth Sahib; arranged marriages.
To understand the way that Sikhs approach death.	The part played by the Guru Granth Sahib; cremation; the Akhand Path.

 # CHRISTIANITY ✝

ONE CHURCH – MANY CHURCHES

► AIMS
1 To introduce the Church as a worldwide organization which takes on many different forms.
2 To introduce the main Christian **denominations**
3 To show the main distinctiveness of the different Churches in the area of worship.

► BACKGROUND INFORMATION

The number of different Christian Churches (denominations) is staggering. There are now thought to be over 20,000 such denominations throughout the world catering for the needs of some 1,200,000,000 worshippers. Many of them have existed for centuries. Others, though, are coming into existence week by week. This is particularly true in Africa where some of the new Churches have a very tenuous connection with historical Christianity.

Amongst the historical denominations there are clear doctrinal differences. The **Church of England, Roman Catholic** and **Orthodox** Churches, for instance, have been historically committed to **infant baptism** and **Confirmation**. They believe that these are **sacraments** which trace their origins back to the Early Church and are the main reason for the Church's existence today. The **Free Churches**, though, do not accept a sacramental style of life nor are most of them committed to either infant baptism or Confirmation. **Baptists**, for example, only baptise adults.

The differences are even more apparent if you look at the styles of worship adopted by the different Churches. Some, like the Roman Catholics and the Anglicans, usually follow set forms of worship laid down in a prayer book. This form of worship is called the **liturgy**. Others feel happier with more informal styles of worship centred around the **Bible**. This is true of the Free Churches.

To make sense of the Christian Church, both in the past and in the present, it is probably necessary to see it as a 'family'. Its various members have disagreed violently and even spilt much blood in the past, but even the Churches which appear to be miles apart have a great deal in common. Many of these differences can be explained by the different cultures in which the various Churches have taken root.

► STARTING POINTS

1 Carry out a small survey of church buildings close to your school. How many different ones can the children find? What are their names?
2 Do the children know what kind of churches they are: Anglican, Catholic, Orthodox, Baptist, Methodist, Salvation Army, etc.?
3 Are any of the churches called by different names: abbey, chapel, citadel, meeting-house? Can you always tell what kind of church it is by its name?
4 Are some churches much older than the others?

► KEY WORDS

Baptist Church; Bible; Church of England; Confirmation; denomination; Free Churches; infant baptism; liturgy; minister; Orthodox Church; pastor; priest; Quakers; Roman Catholic Church; sacrament.

► COPYMASTER

Copymaster 1 Inside a church
This sheet introduces many of the special features that can be found inside a church. Using the Pupils' Book as a guide, the following should be labelled: font, altar, pew, choir, priest, cross, hymn numbers, candles, pulpit. The questions below should then be answered.

✝ CHRISTIANITY

COPYMASTER 1 Name ....

INSIDE A CHURCH

altar; pew; choir; font; pulpit; priest; cross; hymn numbers; candles;

CAN YOU WORK OUT (OR GUESS)?

1 What is usually kept in the font? _____
_____

2 What the choir do in a church service? _____
_____

3 Where the priest stands during a service? _____
_____

4 Whose figure is sometimes on the cross? _____

5 Where the candles are? _____

6 What is read from the lectern in a service? _____

CHRISTIANITY

THE ANGLICAN CHURCH

▶ AIMS
1. To introduce the Anglican Church (The **Church of England** / The Church in Wales).
2. To introduce the Church of England as the most common Church in England.
3. To introduce the baptismal **font**.
4. To introduce stained-glass windows and their original purpose.
5. To introduce the **altar**.
6. To introduce the service of **Holy Communion**.

▶ BACKGROUND INFORMATION

Steps were taken by King Henry VIII in the sixteenth century to break the power that Rome, and the **Pope**, had over the Church in this country. Two Acts of Parliament, in 1536 and 1539, authorised the dissolution of the monasteries. The monasteries were the foundation of Roman Catholic power in this country. The decision was taken to place a copy of the **Bible** in English (this version was known as the Great Bible) in every church. The **Book of Common Prayer**, largely the work of Thomas Cranmer, went through three revisions by 1662. The Book of Common Prayer was the cornerstone of worship in the Church of England until well into the twentieth century. Under Elizabeth I the Church of England became the Established (Official) Church in this country.

The Church of England remains the Established Church. Its leaders are appointed by the Prime Minister. Its **bishops** sit in the House of Lords. Serious changes in the Church, such as the **ordination** of women, have to be debated and passed by Parliament. Its beliefs are still covered by a statement drawn up in the sixteenth century called the **Thirty-nine Articles**.

The Church of England is a 'broad church'. This means that it has different groups within it who believe different things and worship in different ways. Within the modern Church there are three main groups:
- The Low Church or **Evangelicals**,
- The High Church or **Anglo-Catholics**,
- The Liberals.

▶ STARTING POINTS
1. Visit some Church of England buildings. If this can be combined with a service, all the better. Try to find churches which are obviously different, so that an idea of variety can be gained by the children.
2. If possible and appropriate look at the stained-glass windows and do some brass-rubbings with the children.
3. Encourage children to locate the various items mentioned in this spread and others besides.
4. If possible ask the priest to answer questions from the children.

▶ NOTE
For Pupils' Book activity, the story of the Good Samaritan can be found in the Bible at Luke 10.30–37.

▶ KEY WORDS
Altar; Anglo-Catholic; Archbishop of Canterbury; Bible; bishop; Book of Common Prayer; Church of England; Evangelical; font; Holy Communion; Pope; priest; Thirty-nine Articles.

▶ COPYMASTERS
Copymaster 2 Match up in a church
This copymaster will help to reinforce the understanding of the names of various artefacts which are to be found in a church. The definitions should be matched up with the correct words.
Copymaster 3 What you will find in a church
This copymaster will aid understanding of where various artefacts will be found in a church. The illustrations should first be coloured and then cut out and stuck in the correct position on the child's own drawing of the inside of a church. The name of each object should then be written underneath.

✝ CHRISTIANITY

COPYMASTER 2   Name ....

MATCH UP IN A CHURCH

AISLE   The place from which the priest conducts Holy Communion.

PRIEST   The numbers of the hymns in the service.

FONT   The space to walk down between the pews leading towards the altar.

ALTAR   The bowl in which water is kept during infant baptism.

HYMN NUMBERS   The instrument on which music is played.

ORGAN   The person who conducts a service.

CHOIR   The seats on which people sit.

PEWS   The people who sing with and to the people.

CHRISTIANITY ✝

COPYMASTER 3   Name ....

WHAT YOU WILL FIND IN A CHURCH

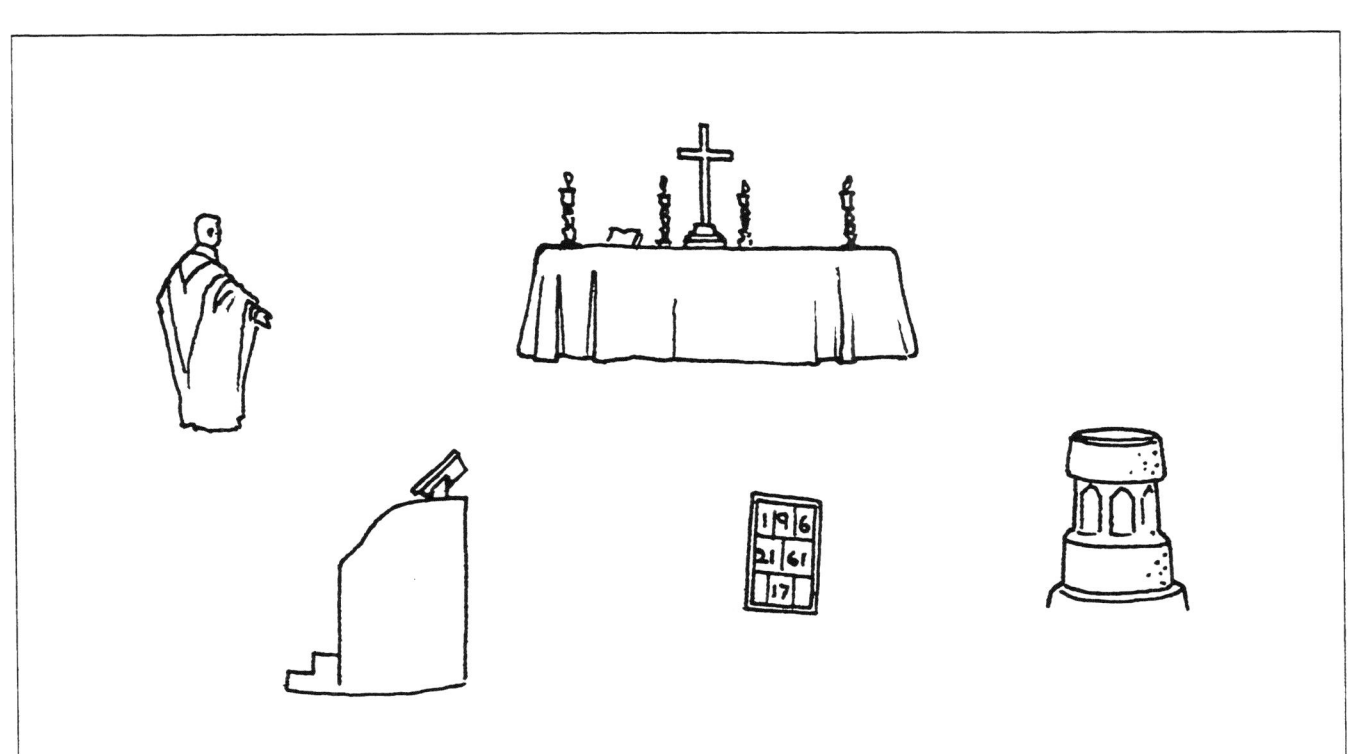

✝ CHRISTIANITY

THE ROMAN CATHOLIC CHURCH

> ▶ AIMS
>
> 1 To introduce the **Roman Catholic Church** as the largest of all the Christian denominations.
> 2 To explain the role of **St Peter** in the Roman Catholic Church.
> 3 To introduce the **Vatican**.
> 4 To introduce the **Pope**.
> 5 To introduce the service of the **Mass**.

▶ BACKGROUND INFORMATION

More Christians throughout the world belong to the Roman Catholic Church than any other. In all, the Church is thought to have some 800,000,000 followers. Roman Catholics trace the origin of their Church back to the words of **Jesus** to Peter in Matthew 16.18: 'And so I tell you, Peter: you are a rock; and on this rock foundation I will build my church, and not even death will ever be able to overcome it.' They take this to mean that Jesus was promising to build his Church on Peter. The same Peter, they believe, became the first **Bishop** of Rome (Pope). The Pope today is still called 'the Bishop of Rome' and has the authority which Jesus gave to Peter. Each Pope has the hands of the **cardinals** 'laid on' him after he has been chosen. In this way the Pope receives the power and authority of the whole Catholic Church, going back directly to St Peter. From time to time he is said to speak '*ex cathedra*' (from the throne) and his words are considered as infallible - direct from God. The Catholic Faith believes that there are seven **sacraments** - special channels of God's grace to believers. They are:
1 **infant baptism**
2 **Confirmation**
3 **Holy Communion**
4 marriage
5 **ordination**
6 **confession**
7 **Sacrament of the sick**

▶ STARTING POINTS

1 Arrange a visit to your local Roman Catholic church. Arrange it at a time when the parish **priest** is available. Ask him to introduce the various artefacts to the children; altar, reserved sacrament, holy water, crucifix, statues of Mary, etc. Encourage the children to ask their own questions.
2 Put together a montage of photographs of people, objects, etc., linked with the Roman Catholic Church.

▶ KEY WORDS

Bishop; cardinal; confession; Confirmation; disciple; heaven; Holy Communion; infant baptism; Mass; ordination; St Peter; Pope; Roman Catholic Church; sacrament; Sacrament of the sick; Vatican.

▶ COPYMASTERS

Copymaster 4 In a Roman Catholic church
This sheet introduces some of the items specific to the Roman Catholic Church alongside those which are common to many churches. Best effect can be gained from this sheet by using it on (or after) a visit to a Roman Catholic church. Name the arrowed objects in the illustration: altar, crucifix, candles, statue of the Virgin Mary, reserved sacrament, priest.

 **CHRISTIANITY** ✝

COPYMASTER 4   Name ....

IN A ROMAN CATHOLIC CHURCH

The name of the Roman Catholic church is _____
_____

The name of the parish priest is _____
_____

He is called 'Father' because _____
_____

7

✝ CHRISTIANITY

THE METHODIST CHURCH

> ► AIMS
> 1 To introduce **John Wesley** who is one of the most important English religious leaders.
> 2 To introduce Wesley's missionary travels.
> 3 To show the link between Wesley and the beginning of the **Methodist Church**.
> 4 To underline the close link between the Methodist Church and the great tradition of hymn-writing and hymn-singing.

► BACKGROUND INFORMATION

John Wesley first received the name 'Methodist' whilst studying at Oxford because of the methodical way that he studied and read the **Bible**. He was ordained in the **Church of England** on leaving university, but without any strong personal religious convictions. He had a spiritual 'conversion' experience in his mid-thirties in which he described his heart as being 'strangely warmed'. He was convinced that Christ had taken away his sins and that he was 'saved'.
Bolstered by this new-found religious assurance he set out across England on horseback to bring the message of salvation to the masses. To begin with he preached in Church of England churches but he soon found that these opportunities were increasingly denied to him, as others in the Church of England were unhappy with his 'conversion' experience. He began to preach in the open air as he could not preach in churches. It is estimated that he must have ridden over 100,000 miles in the course of a very long ministry. Thousands of people were converted to Christianity through his preaching.
Because of the opposition from the Church of England, Wesley began to develop a separate organisation within which to work. This movement, the Methodist Church, began to build its own **chapels** and ordain its own **ministers**.

► STARTING POINTS

1 Talk with the children about eighteenth-century Britain; poor communications, roads, etc.
2 Talk about the problems of travelling long distances on horseback; highwaymen, disease, hunger, etc.
3 Ask them to imagine what it was like for Wesley to arrive in a totally strange place; the opposition that he met and where it came from, etc.; what drove Wesley and his friends on.

► KEY WORDS

Bible; chapel; Church of England; Methodist Church; minister; John Wesley.

► COPYMASTER

Copymaster 5 John Wesley and the early Methodists
This sheet underlines the details of the story of John Wesley and the foundation of the Methodist movement. Colour in the central picture of John Wesley disputing with some colleagues. Write underneath the three drawings describing what is happening. Ask the children to draw their own pictures to show an aspect of early Methodism. Ask them to describe what is happening in their own pictures.

CHRISTIANITY ✝

COPYMASTER 5   Name ....

JOHN WESLEY AND THE EARLY METHODISTS

✝ CHRISTIANITY

THE SALVATION ARMY

> ► AIMS
> 1 To introduce the most visible of the Christian Churches: the **Salvation Army**.
> 2 To introduce the distinctive uniform of the Salvation Army.
> 3 To introduce the work of the Salvation Army amongst the disadvantaged in society.
> 4 To show the distinctiveness of Salvation Army worship.
> 5 To introduce the name for a Salvation Army place of worship: the **citadel**.

► BACKGROUND INFORMATION

The Salvation Army is a **Protestant** Christian movement which was begun by William and Catherine Booth in London in 1877. The intention of Booth was to care for, and convert, London's poor to the Christian Gospel since they were being neglected by Christianity's more mainline denominations. He organised his new evangelistic movement along military lines with himself as 'general' supported by 'colonels', 'adjutants' and 'corporals'. Within a short time the Salvation Army had achieved a large following, with many people involved in social and religious work in Britain and elsewhere.

In worship the Salvation Army pioneered mass meetings in the open air. Brass bands were soon formed and these became a real focus of attention in Victorian Britain. At the same time the Salvation Army devoted considerable energy to various social outcasts. In particular, early Salvationists concentrated their energies on men who had been released from prison. Homes for needy women and children, and for ex-prisoners, were built with money raised through appeals and the selling of the Salvation Army's newspaper, the *War Cry*.

The Salvation Army continues to hold to a largely Puritanical approach to morality. Salvationists have always spoken out against the evils of alcohol, so teetotalism is required of all officers. Smoking is forbidden. Officers are only allowed to marry other officers.

► STARTING POINTS

1 Salvation Army officers are amongst the most accessible of Church representatives. There is a welter of material available about the Army and the work that it does. The Salvation Army has a very practical way of working out its Christianity, so it is possible to talk extensively about that work in a way that is easy to understand.
2 Talk about the most needy people in modern society: alcoholics, the homeless, ex-prisoners, those who have left home, etc. Look at two of these groups more closely. How did they come to be as they are? What help do they need? Why do they need help? What help is the Salvation Army able to provide?
3 If you can, invite a Salvation Army officer in to talk to the class about their work. (This ties in with one of the activities suggested in the 'Things to do' section of the Pupils' Book.)

► KEYWORDS

Citadel; Protestant; Salvation Army.

► COPYMASTERS

Copymaster 6 The Salvation Army officer
This copymaster reinforces recognition of the unique Salvation Army uniform, and the way of life of a Salvation Army officer. Colour in the drawing of the Salvation Army officer using photographs from Pupils' Book to help. Write three sentences about the life of a Salvation Army officer.

Copymaster 7 Working with the Salvation Army
This copymaster underlines the practical work of the Salvation Army. Draw small pictures in the boxes to show five different kinds of people that the Salvation Army officer helps. Describe underneath how you think these people might be helped.

CHRISTIANITY ✝

COPYMASTER 6   Name ....

THE SALVATION ARMY OFFICER

THE LIFE OF A SALVATION ARMY OFFICER

_____
_____
_____
_____
_____
_____
_____
_____

CHRISTIANITY

COPYMASTER 7   Name ....

THE WORK OF A SALVATION ARMY OFFICER

CHRISTIANITY

THE ORTHODOX CHURCH

> ► AIMS
> 1 To introduce an unfamiliar wing of the Christian Church, the **Orthodox Church**.
> 2 To hint at the beauty which is an integral part of the Orthodox worship and its buildings.
> 3 To introduce **icons**.

► BACKGROUND INFORMATION

Some 150,000,000 people belong to the Orthodox Church in Russia, Eastern Europe and the Eastern Mediterranean. These Christians belong to a Church which goes back to the very origins of Christianity itself. The Church is divided into two main groups or families of Churches:
1 The Oriental Orthodox Church with about 30,000,000 believers.
2 The Eastern Orthodox Church which has about 120,000,000 believers.
The Orthodox Church believes that:
- God is a Trinity; three persons within the single godhead.
- **Jesus** Christ was fully God and fully human.
- The Church spans both **heaven** and earth. Jesus Christ, the Apostles and the martyrs form the Church's foundation. All believers join with them in the one Church.
- All worship must centre around the **sacraments**, or 'mysteries', of which there are seven. The **Divine Liturgy** is the most important service of the week.
- Men and women must worship God with all their senses. The Divine Liturgy service makes full use of **incense**, the chanting voice of the **priest**, the songs of the choir and the unaccompanied reply of the congregation. Icons also play a very important role in religious devotion. During a service worshippers move around in front of them bowing and kissing them as a mark of respect.

► STARTING POINTS

Orthodox worship places a very high degree of importance on the senses. Try to convey something of this to the children. Visit an Orthodox church if this is possible. It is most effective when a service is going on, but an Orthodox church does have a unique atmosphere at any time. Failing this, try to use large photographs, artefacts, tapes of music, etc., to give some idea of the feeling in an Orthodox church. Talk about the importance of atmosphere. What sort of atmosphere does an Orthodox building, and act of worship, attempt to create?

► KEY WORDS

Altar; Divine Liturgy; heaven; icon; iconostasis; incense; Jesus; Orthodox Church; priest; sacrament; saint; Virgin Mary.

► COPYMASTER

Copymaster 8 The iconostasis
This copymaster will help pupils to understand what icons and the **iconostasis** look like, as well as the position and function of the iconostasis in the church. Pupils should copy the pictures of icons from the lower picture on to the picture of the iconostasis in the spaces provided. The priest should be visible at the altar through the door of the iconostasis.

CHRISTIANITY

COPYMASTER 8

Name ....

THE ICONOSTASIS

# CHRISTIANITY ✝

CONFIRMATION

> ► AIMS
> 1 To show the close link that exists between **infant baptism** and **Confirmation**.
> 2 To show that Confirmation is an important Christian rite in Churches which also perform infant baptism. In practice this means the **Church of England** and the **Roman Catholic Church**.
> 3 To show the importance which these two Churches attach to Confirmation; underlined by the fact that it is always performed by a **bishop**.
> 4 To show the importance of the **laying on of hands**; the historical and symbolic means by which the **Holy Spirit** is given to people.

► BACKGROUND

1 In the **Orthodox Church** baptism, Confirmation (called **Chrismation**) and the first **Holy Communion** all take place at the same time. Although provision is made in the Roman Catholic Church to confirm older people it is normally carried out from the age of seven onwards. The Church of England usually confirms teenagers although older people are frequently confirmed.
2 The laying on of hands is the most important aspect of every Confirmation service. Many Christians believe that bishops can trace their authority, through the constant laying on of hands, back to the original Apostles. This gives them the unique authority to bestow the gift of the Holy Spirit on others. The Roman Catholic Church is committed most heavily to this view with the bishop telling each confirmand: 'Be sealed with the Holy Spirit.'
3 Although **Nonconformist** Churches rarely confirm, some of them do have their own equivalents. The **Baptist Church** extends 'the right hand of fellowship' to those recently baptised as adults. In the **Methodist Church** a public reception into full membership involves the laying on of the **minister**'s hands. Members of the Methodist Church sign a membership card and renew their membership each year at a special service.

► STARTING POINTS

1 Talk about infant baptism. Normally, how old is the baby when he or she is baptised? How much can the baby understand of the event? What is the value of other people making promises on their behalf? What are the disadvantages of this? Give examples of decisions that adults take for children: choice of school, etc.
2 Take the discussion on a stage further and talk about the 'age of responsibility'. When are we old enough to take our own decisions? What decisions can the children in the class take for themselves? What does the law say? What about 'spiritual' decisions? What kind of decisions fall into this category? Talk about the difference in ages at which the Catholic and the Anglican Churches are willing to confirm.

► KEY WORDS

Baptist Church; bishop; chrismation; Church of England; Confirmation; Holy Communion; Holy Spirit; infant baptism; laying on of hands; Methodist Church; minister; Nonconformist Church; priest; Roman Catholic Church; sign of the cross.

► COPYMASTERS

Copymaster 9 Being confirmed
This copymaster looks at the main people involved in a Confirmation service and its relationship with the earlier service of child baptism. Answer questions on sheet. Colour in drawing of bishop.
Copymaster 10 The Confirmation service
This sheet reinforces knowledge of the sequence of events in a Confirmation service and understanding of it. Cut out the four drawings. Colour each of the drawings. Drawings to be pasted down in the order in which they occur in the Confirmation service. A maximum of three sentences to be written by each drawing to describe what is happening.

✝ CHRISTIANITY

COPYMASTER 9 Name ....

BEING CONFIRMED

'...at your baptism you were received into God's family, the Church. You have grown in the knowledge and love of our Lord. You have heard Christ saying "Follow me" as he said to his first disciples. You have already responded to his call and you come now by your own choice to renounce evil and profess your faith in him. You are now to be confirmed...'

1 Who speaks these words? _____

2 Who is he speaking to? _____

3 Who made the promises when the person was baptised? _____
   _____

4 What is the difference between baptism and Confirmation? _____
   _____

CHRISTIANITY ✝

COPYMASTER 10 Name ....

THE CONFIRMATION SERVICE

✝ CHRISTIANITY

ADULT BAPTISM

> ► AIMS
> 1 To introduce **adult baptism** as distinct from **infant baptism**.
> 2 To introduce the alternative names for adult baptism: **Believer's Baptism** and **baptism by immersion**.
> 3 To show the link between adult baptism and the **Baptist Church**.
> 4 To show the connection between adult baptism and the baptism of **Jesus**.
> 5 To introduce the various stages of adult baptism.

► BACKGROUND INFORMATION

Some Christian Churches, most notably but not exclusively the Baptist Church, do not believe that it is appropriate to baptise babies. They argue that someone should only be baptised if they believe in and understand the Christian faith for themselves.

The strongest motivation for many Christians to be baptised is the example of Jesus who was baptised in the River Jordan by **John the Baptist**. The practice is also tied in closely with the death, burial and resurrection of Jesus.

Stage one: going down into the water symbolises the person leaving their old life, with all its sinful ways, behind them. In religious language they are 'dying to sin'. A parallel is drawn between the death of Jesus on the cross and this symbolic 'death' of each believer.

Stage two: being immersed beneath the water symbolises that the person has broken with their old life; they are 'buried' with Christ.

Stage three: coming up out of the water, and leaving the pool by different steps, symbolises that they are sharing in the 'resurrection life' of Christ. They believe that just as Jesus was brought back from the dead to share God's new life so are they doing the same spiritually.

► STARTING POINTS

1 Water is a very important religious symbol, and baptism is found in other religions – Judaism and Sikhism – as well as Christianity. Give examples of the different uses to which water is put: to give life, to refresh, to cleanse, etc. Talk about a shortage of water – drought.
2 Look at baptism from the point of view of an adult about to be baptised. Why are they being baptised? What is the importance of the ceremony for them? Do they have a Christian faith already? Why do they feel that obedience is important?
3 If you can, invite a Baptist **pastor** into the class to talk about adult baptism. (This ties in with one of the activities suggested in the 'Things to do' section of the Pupils' Book.)

► KEYWORDS

Adult baptism; Baptist Church; baptism by immersion; Believer's Baptism; Jesus; John the Baptist; pastor.

► COPYMASTERS

Copymaster 11 Adult baptism – what is happening?
This sheet reinforces understanding of adult baptism; its significance and symbolism. Answer the questions on the sheet. Then colour the drawings. Describe what is happening in each drawing.

 **CHRISTIANITY** ✝

COPYMASTER 11　　　　　　　Name ....

ADULT BAPTISM – WHAT IS HAPPENING?

Adult baptism is _____
_____

This scene is probably taking place in _____

To be baptised as an adult someone must _____
_____

_____
_____
_____

_____
_____
_____

_____
_____
_____

_____
_____
_____

✝ CHRISTIANITY

MARRIAGE

> ► AIMS
>
> 1 To show that Christians see marriage as a gift from God for the human race.
> 2 To explain that marriage has two purposes: that two people can share their lives together, that children can be brought up within a family atmosphere.
> 3 To show that during the Christian marriage ceremony the man and the woman promise to share their lives and to love one another 'till death us do part'.
> 4 To show that the giving and the receiving of a ring or rings is a visible sign of the couple's love for each other.

► BACKGROUND INFORMATION

To the **Roman Catholic Church** marriage is one of seven **sacraments**. Other Christian Churches do not see it in quite the same terms. For them marriage is a solemn agreement in God's sight between a man and a woman who love each other. Their love for each other reflects the love which, in the **Bible**, **Jesus** is said to have for his 'bride', the Church.
Although wedding services differ from Church to Church they have a common basis.
- The wedding takes place in the sight of God and in front of friends and relations. Whilst there must be at least two human witnesses to every wedding, the witness who Christians consider really matters is God.
- The marriage is a lifelong commitment between the man and the woman, although all Churches, apart from the Roman Catholic Church, officially recognise divorce.
- Every marriage can expect to be blessed with the gift of children, although 1 in every 10 marriages is childless.

During the church service the **priest** or **minister** gives three reasons why marriage is important:
1 So that the two people can love and comfort each other.
2 To provide the most secure and loving environment in which sexual intercourse can take place.
3 To provide a loving and caring home into which children can be born and brought up.

► STARTING POINTS

1 Talk about different kinds of rings: engagement, wedding, eternity rings, etc. Why are they amongst the most popular of all visible symbols? Do they always symbolise love? Why might people sometimes need the reminder provided by such a visible symbol?
2 Talk about any weddings that members of the class have been to recently. Have any been to weddings either in a **Registry Office** or a place of worship other than a church? Ask them to describe the wedding. Why do some people choose not to marry in a church? What are the essential differences between the different kinds of weddings?

► KEY WORDS

Bible; Jesus; minister; mosque; priest; Registry Office; Roman Catholic Church; sacrament; synagogue.

► COPYMASTERS

Copymaster 12 A Christian wedding
This sheet reinforces understanding of the wedding service. Look at each of the five picture squares. Think of the part that each of them plays in a Christian wedding service. Cut out each of the drawings and match them with the comments to make an information sheet on 'a Christian wedding'. Write a description of a Christian wedding, mentioning the different events described on the sheet.

CHRISTIANITY

COPYMASTER 12   Name ....

A CHRISTIAN WEDDING

The priest talks to the couple and they make promises to each other.

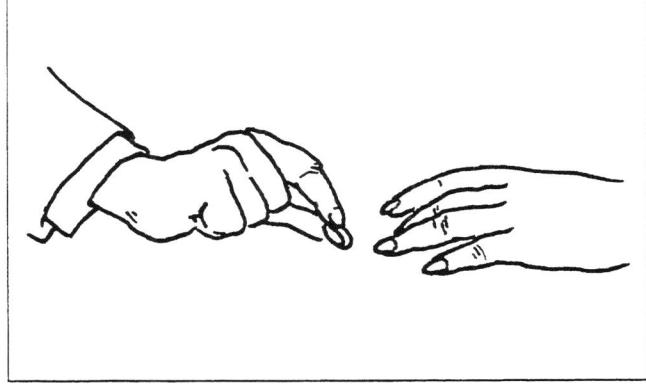

The bride comes down the aisle holding the arm of her father. The bridesmaids walk behind her.

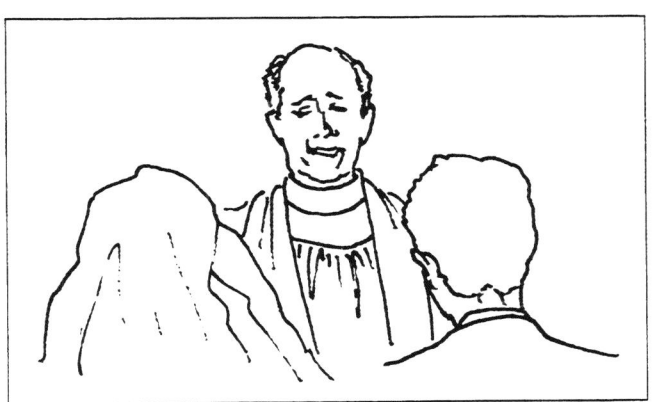

The couple sign their names in the marriage register. Two witnesses must also sign their names.

The groom puts a ring on the finger of his bride. This reminds them of their love for each other.

The couple leave the church arm in arm. Their friends and relatives follow behind.

✝ CHRISTIANITY

DEATH

> ▶ AIMS
> 1 To introduce the idea of death in a caring and sympathetic environment. (Obviously teachers must be sensitive to any situations in which death has affected someone in the class.)
> 2 To introduce the practice, found particularly in the **Roman Catholic Church**, of the **Sacrament of the sick**.
> 3 To describe a Christian funeral and burial.

▶ BACKGROUND INFORMATION

The Christian Church has always held strongly developed ideas about death and life after death. These are reflected in the different funeral services in the various Christian **denominations**. These services may vary in detail, but they are in agreement about the basic beliefs. The underlying belief is the conviction that death is the gateway to something eternal. The physical part of a person, the body, decays and returns to dust, but the spiritual, the **soul**, survives for ever.

The Christian funeral service stresses the belief that **Jesus** rose from the dead, and that all believers will do likewise. Christianity believes in a physical resurrection of the body when Christ returns to the earth.

Roman Catholics believe that most souls spend time in **purgatory** before reaching **heaven**. They believe that purgatory is a place of refinement. It is natural, therefore, for them to pray for the soul of the person while it is there. Prayers are said for the dead at every **Mass**.

Protestants do not believe in purgatory. When a person has died they commit his or her soul to God's safe keeping through a series of **Bible** readings and prayers.

Christian believers look forward to the 'end of time' when they believe that they will be given a 'new body' similar to the one that Christ had after his resurrection.

▶ STARTING POINTS

1 Sensitively explore any experience that the children might have had of death: the death of a grandparent, or death of a pet, etc. Encourage the children to talk about the experience. Introduce the idea that in the end everything, and everyone, dies. Take examples of this from the natural world: animals, insects, plants, etc.
2 Talk about the idea of a life span. Why is the life span of some forms of nature so short?
3 Can the worth or value of any form of life be gauged by the length of time that it survives? What makes a life really valuable? How does this value survive after the life ends?

▶ KEYWORDS

Bible; heaven; Jesus; Mass; Protestants; purgatory; Roman Catholic Church; Sacrament of the sick; soul.

▶ COPYMASTER

Copymaster 13 The Twenty-third Psalm

This copymaster introduces the the Twenty-third Psalm, and aims to show how people draw comfort from this psalm. Go through the psalm with children explaining what it means where necessary. Ask children to draw illustrations to go with phrases of the psalm and then ask them to explain why they think the psalm is used at many Christian funerals.

CHRISTIANITY

COPYMASTER 13

Name ....

THE TWENTY-THIRD PSALM

The Twenty-third Psalm is read at many Christian funerals. It is very special to most Christians. Try drawing some pictures to go with the words.

'The Lord is my shepherd; I have everything I need. He lets me rest in fields of green grass . . .'

'. . . and leads me to quiet pools of fresh water. He gives me new strength. He guides me in the right paths, as he has promised.'

'Even if I go through the deepest darkness, I will not be afraid, Lord . . .'

'. . . for you are with me. Your shepherd's rod and staff protect me.'

I think that this Psalm is read at most Christian funerals because

_____
_____
_____
_____
_____

✡ JUDAISM

THE TEN SAYINGS

> ► AIMS
> 1 To introduce the **Ten Sayings**.
> 2 To introduce the **Torah** as a whole with its 613 laws.
> 3 To introduce **Moses** as the great law-giver of the **Jews**.

► BACKGROUND INFORMATION

The Ten Sayings (Commandments) are at the very heart of the Jewish faith. Nine of them are in the form of commands. The first saying is a statement that all of the commands come from God, who frees people from slavery and gives them the opportunity to choose goodness.

Judaism has never separated ethical and moral behaviour from religion. Jews were called to turn all people away from violence and inhumanity, but not in preparation for a future life of eternal bliss. It is the establishment of a kingdom of peace and harmony on earth that all Jews are called to work towards. The historical situation in which the Ten Sayings were delivered is very important. The Jews had recently left Egypt after over 400 years of slavery. Their wanderings through the wilderness appeared to be largely aimless, until they arrived at the foot of Mount Sinai. Once there Moses informed the Israelites that he must climb the mountain to meet with God. In the Jewish **Scriptures** mountains are almost invariably the place where God chooses to reveal himself to the people. Mountains have obvious links with height and by extension **heaven** and mystery.

The Ten Sayings fall naturally into two groups:
1 Sayings 1-4 are theological, describing God as the one who delivered the Jews from slavery in Egypt. As such he was not prepared to tolerate them worshipping any other deities (gods). He also demanded great respect for **Shabbat** (the holy day) and his own name. These sayings express a mixture of love and fear of God.
2 Sayings 5-10 deal with relationships between people. They provide a means of expressing the love of the Israelites for God in concrete human action.

The Ten Sayings make it clear that no one can claim to love God and yet do anything to hurt their neighbour at the same time.

► STARTING POINTS

1 Put the Ten Sayings into context. The Israelites had left Egypt after 400 years of slavery and had become nomads. All the time, though, their number was growing. Smaller tribes were joining them for some measure of protection. They had no organisation or rules to guarantee their survival.
2 Find a parallel to help the children understand this. Try the example of a new school in which the headteacher and staff meet to decide what rules the school is going to need. Why are rules necessary in the first place? What is the difference between commands and rules? What rules will be needed?
3 Imagine the situation of the Israelites. What were the main problems faced? What rules (commands) were needed to safeguard them and their future?

► KEY WORDS

Bible; Jew; heaven; Moses; Torah; Scriptures; Shabbat; synagogue; Ten Commandments; Ten Sayings.

► COPYMASTERS

Copymaster 14 Receiving the Ten Sayings
This sheet puts the giving of the Ten Sayings into the context in which the events are said to have taken place. Colour the drawings and then cut them out. Paste drawings down in their correct order. Write four sentences to describe the sequence of pictures.

Copymaster 15 The Ten Sayings
This copymaster focuses on the Ten Sayings themselves and the Israelites' relationship with God. Copy out the Ten Sayings. Answer the questions on the sheet about commandments.

JUDAISM

COPYMASTER 14   Name ....

RECEIVING THE TEN SAYINGS

1)

2)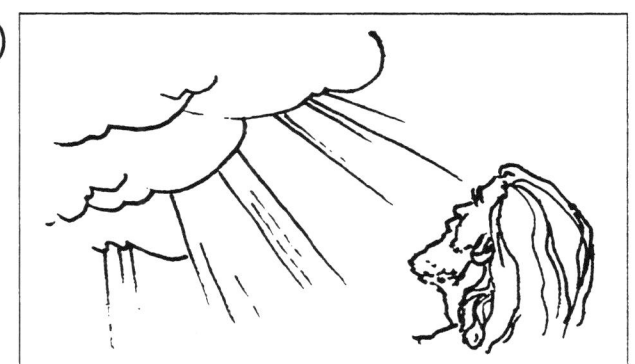

3)

4)

5)

6)

✡ JUDAISM   ✡ ☪ ✝ ☬

COPYMASTER 15   Name ....

THE TEN SAYINGS

1 Where were the Israelites travelling from when they received the Ten Sayings? _____

2 Where did the Israelites rest on their journey? _____

3 Who left everyone else and climbed up on to a mountain?
   _____

4 Who did the leader of the Israelites meet on the mountain?
   _____

5 What was given by God on the mountain? (Careful!)
   _____

6 Who are the first four sayings all about (apart from the Israelites)?
   _____

7 Who are the last six sayings all about? _____

JUDAISM

AROUND BIRTH

▶ AIMS
1. To highlight the excitement which **Jews** feel over the birth of a new baby. This excitement is greatly increased by the Jewish conviction that the child is a gift from God.
2. To draw attention to the difference between the way that the birth of a boy and the birth of a girl are celebrated in the Jewish community.
3. To introduce **circumcision** (**Brit Millah**) as a very important Jewish ritual.
4. To link circumcision with the covenant (agreement) that God made with **Abraham** in the Jewish **Scriptures**.

▶ BACKGROUND INFORMATION

According to the book of Genesis the decision to circumcise all male Jews was first taken after a conversation between God and Abraham. This makes circumcision the oldest Jewish tradition of all. Abraham was told that circumcision is a physical sign of the covenant between God and the Jewish people. A man cannot be a Jew unless he is circumcised.

- Circumcision is always carried out on a Jewish boy on the eighth day after he is born. The same tradition is found in Islam.
- Just as Abraham was responsible for circumcising all the males in his household so the Jewish father has traditionally been responsible for circumcising his sons. For a long time, however, people called '**mohalim**' have been specially trained to carry out this delicate task.
- After the child has been circumcised the baby's father says:

"Praised be Thou, O Lord our God, ruling spirit of the universe, who has commanded us to enter into the covenant of our father, Abraham."

The people then reply:

"As he (the child) has entered into the covenant, so may he enter into love of the **Torah**, into the marriage canopy and into the life of good deeds."

The baby is given his name and a drop of wine is placed on his lips. The father drinks the remainder of the glass.

What does circumcision mean for a Jew? A baby boy is a Jew primarily because he has a Jewish mother and not because he is circumcised. His circumcision, however, does have two important implications:
1. The baby receives his father's blessing and, since the time of Abraham, this has been very important.
2. The baby becomes 'ritually clean' and is welcomed into the Jewish community. The 'sign' in his flesh will constantly remind him of this.

If the baby is a girl, the father is given the honour of reading from the Torah in the **synagogue** on the next **Shabbat** morning. He will also announce the baby's name to everyone.

▶ STARTING POINTS
1. Talk about the different ways that people in this country celebrate the birth of a baby: cards, Christening, etc. Why is birth looked upon as such an important event? What impact does the birth of a baby have upon other members of the family?
2. Talk about 'signs of membership'. Religious signs: baptism, etc. Other signs in Brownies, Cubs, etc. Why are such 'signs' important? Why should Jewish men have such an indelible sign that they belong to the Jewish people?

▶ KEY WORDS
Abraham; Brit Millah; circumcision; Jew; mohel; Scriptures; Shabbat; synagogue; Torah.

▶ COPYMASTER
Copymaster 16 Around birth
This copymaster concentrates on the welcome into the world given to a Jewish child. Answer the questions.

JUDAISM

COPYMASTER 16

Name ....

AROUND BIRTH

Answer each of these questions:

1 How is a baby girl welcomed into the Jewish community?

   _____

   _____

2 Who announces the name of a baby girl and where?

   _____

   _____

3 When is a baby boy circumcised?

   _____

   _____

4 Who was first told by God to circumcise his family?

   _____

   _____

JUDAISM

BARMITZVAH AND BATMITZVAH

> ▶ AIMS
> 1 To introduce the very important Jewish ceremony of **barmitzvah** and the less important **batmitzvah**.
> 2 To introduce the Sunday School; an important part of the learning process for all young **Jews**. Judaism places a very heavy emphasis upon learning – at all ages.
> 3 To underline the honour that is felt at being invited to read the **Torah** in public in the **synagogue**.

▶ BACKGROUND INFORMATION

During his religious education a Jewish boy is introduced to the **mitzvot** (commandments) which outline his duties and responsibilities when he becomes an adult. The Jewish community considers that adulthood begins for him when he reaches his thirteenth birthday. The occasion is marked by him becoming a barmitzvah – a 'son of the commandment'.

In the ceremony held in the synagogue on the first **Shabbat** after his thirteenth birthday, several important events take place:

- The boy is called forward, for the first time, to read in **Hebrew** from the **Sefer Torah**. As this privilege is only extended to adult males in the Jewish Orthodox community, this is a public recognition that the boy has come of age.
- The boy receives his father's blessing. This has always been important in Judaism. The father thanks God that he has now been relieved of the responsibility of his son's spiritual welfare.
- The parents arrange a meal which is eaten after the ceremony. This meal is called the seudah.

From this time onwards the boy is allowed to wear his **tallit** and **tefillin**. The occasion also provides the opportunity for the boy to renew his dedication to the Jewish faith – just as **Confirmation** does for Christians and joining the **Khalsa** does for Sikhs.

Orthodox synagogues do have a female equivalent to barmitzvah (called **Bat Hayil** – daughter of valour) but reading from the Torah is not allowed. In Reform synagogues, however, there is a much closer equivalent to barmitzvah – called 'batmitzvah'. This means the 'daughter of the commandment'. During this service girls do read from the Torah in public – just as women do in ordinary worship in Reform synagogues.

▶ STARTING POINTS

1 Talk about the different roles given to men and women within the Jewish community. Those within the Jewish Orthodox community would argue that a woman's main area of influence is the home. This spills over into the fact that there is no serious equivalent to barmitzvah for girls in Orthodox synagogues.
2 Talk about the importance of learning. What do children learn at school? What do children learn at home? Do they learn things elsewhere? Why do Jewish people think additional lessons for Jewish children important? What are they expected to learn in Sunday Schools?
3 Discuss the importance of marking the transition from childhood to adulthood with a ceremony. When do children think that this transition takes place? What about the teenage years? Why are they not recognised within the Jewish community? Is the age of thirteen about right?

▶ KEY WORDS

Abraham; barmitzvah; batmitzvah; Bat Hayil; David; Hebrew; mitzvot; Moses; Scriptures; Sefer Torah; Shabbat; synagogue; tallit; tefillin; Torah; yad.

▶ COPYMASTER

Copymaster 17 The barmitzvah
This copymaster helps identify various important artefacts to be found in Jewish worship which are important parts of the barmitzvah ceremony. Identify and name: Torah, yad, tallit and yarmulka. Write a sentence about each.

JUDAISM

COPYMASTER 17

Name ....

THE BARMITZVAH

1 What is the name of the scroll the boy is reading? _____
_____

2 What is the name of the pointer people use to help them read the text? _____
_____

3 What is the name of the shawl which is worn? _____
_____

4 What is the name of the hat that the boy is wearing? _____
_____

30

JUDAISM

ROSH HASHANAH AND YOM KIPPUR

> ► AIMS
> 1 To introduce the Jewish festivals of **Rosh Hashanah** and **Yom Kippur**.
> 2 To show that heart-searching and repentance for past sins is an integral part of Jewish worship.
> 3 To introduce the **shofar**.

► BACKGROUND

The Jewish New Year, Rosh Hashanah, along with Yom Kippur, the **Day of Atonement**, are the most solemn days in the Jewish year. They fall in the seventh month of the Jewish calendar, Tishri (September/October), and are marked by ten days of heart-searching and repentance. Many **Jews** celebrate Rosh Hashanah over two days instead of one.

Rosh Hashanah
The main symbol of Rosh Hashanah is the ram's horn – the shofar. During the main service in the **synagogue** on Rosh Hashanah the shofar is blown 100 times. Just as trumpets are blown to announce the coming of a human king so the shofar announces the coronation of God. It also calls the people to:
- Look back to the creation of the world when God made all things perfectly.
- Look forward to the time of judgement when God will call on all people to account for the way that they have lived.

Yom Kippur
The holiest day in the Jewish calendar when all Jews are called upon to 'afflict their souls' by abstaining from all food and drink. The only exceptions are children and those who are too ill to **fast**. During the day, which is spent mainly in the synagogue, Jews seek the forgiveness of God and of each other. Five services take place on this day – the first being *Kol Nidre* and the last *Neilah*.

► STARTING POINTS

1 What do the children do when they feel extremely sorry for something they have done? How do they seek forgiveness? How important is it to be forgiven? Why is saying sorry a vital part of finding forgiveness? May something else sometimes be required – restitution? Why do Jews seek forgiveness from God and others on Rosh Hashanah?
2 Arrange a visit from a **rabbi** or someone else from the synagogue. Ask them to bring a shofar along with them. Listen to a demonstration of the different sounds. Ask the children to look for the links between the sounds and the feelings they are intended to suggest. Find out just why the shofar is blown on Rosh Hashanah.

► KEY WORDS

Day of Atonement; fast; heaven; Jew; rabbi; Rosh Hashanah; shofar; synagogue; Yom Kippur.

► COPYMASTER

Copymaster 18 Blowing the shofar
This sheet helps explore the festival of Rosh Hashanah, and the significance of the shofar and the different sounds it makes. Colour in the drawing of the man blowing the shofar in the synagogue on Rosh Hashanah. Describe the different sounds made by the shofar. Explain the reasons for the different sounds.

JUDAISM

COPYMASTER 18 Name ....

BLOWING THE SHOFAR

SOUND ONE
What does it sound like? _____

_____

What does it mean? _____

_____

SOUND TWO
What does it sound like? _____

_____

What does it mean? _____

_____

SOUND THREE
What does it sound like? _____

_____

What does it mean? _____

_____

JUDAISM

MARRIAGE

> ► AIMS
> 1 To introduce the idea of marriage within the Jewish community as a gift from God.
> 2 To see the **ketubah** as a very important part of the Jewish religious tradition.
> 3 To draw out the important symbolism in the Jewish wedding service – such as the **huppah**.

► BACKGROUND

According to Jewish religious tradition marriage is God's plan for the human race – as shown by the first man and woman in the Garden of Eden in the book of Genesis. Jewish people believe that marriage is both the means to personal fulfilment and a sacred bond between three people: God, the man and the woman. The purpose of marriage is to build a home, create a family and play a part in perpetuating the Jewish faith.

Jewish weddings do not have to be conducted in a **synagogue** by a **rabbi**. In practice, though, in this country they usually are. They also follow a similar pattern:

- Both the bride and the groom **fast** before the service. This allows them to seek God's forgiveness for any past mistakes and provides them with the opportunity of starting afresh in their married life together.
- The ketubah must be signed before the service by the groom in the presence of two male witnesses. This is a formal contract which outlines what will happen if the groom divorces his wife or dies before she does.
- The performance of the wedding ceremony under the huppah. This is a symbol of the home that the two of them are going to set up together. Under the huppah they drink two shared glasses of wine together to symbolise their shared destiny. The groom also places a simple gold ring on the forefinger of the bride's left hand.
- The ketubah is read out in public before being handed to the bride. The 'seven blessings of wedlock' are chanted ending with the words: 'Blessed art Thou, O Lord, who gladdens the bridegroom with the bride.'
- The bridegroom then crushes a wineglass beneath his feet to the sound of 'Mazel Tov' (Good Luck). Apart from symbolising the good and bad times ahead in their marriage the broken glass also looks back to the destruction of the **Temple** in **Jerusalem** by the Babylonians in 586 BCE.

► STARTING POINTS

1 Discuss with the children any wedding that they have been to. Where was it held? In a religious building or a **Registry Office**? What was distinctive about it? What did the people wear? What words were said? Were any symbolic actions performed? Was it similar – or different – to a Jewish wedding? What is distinctive about a Jewish wedding?
2 Talk about the use of symbolism in wedding services. Go through some common pieces of symbolism: dress, ring, etc. Why are they important? Isolate those pieces of symbolism in a Jewish wedding. What do they mean?

► KEY WORDS

Fast; huppah; Jerusalem; ketubah; rabbi; Registry Office; Shabbat; synagogue; Talmud; Temple; yarmulka.

► COPYMASTER

Copymaster 19 A Jewish wedding
This copymaster will help identify various important objects used in the Jewish wedding ceremony, and their significance. Identify each of the drawings at the top of the sheet. Describe each drawing in the spaces provided.

JUDAISM

COPYMASTER 19 Name ....

A JEWISH WEDDING

1 The huppah _____
_____
_____

2 The ketubah _____
_____
_____

3 Ring _____
_____
_____

4 Wine glass _____
_____
_____

5 People shouting _____
_____
_____

JUDAISM

DEATH

> ▶ AIMS
> 1 To show that Jewish people believe that each person has been allotted a life span by God. He controls human destiny.
> 2 To show that those approaching death take time to pray that their sins might be forgiven.
> 3 To show how the close relatives of the one who dies express their feelings of grief.
> 4 To introduce the work of the **Chevra Kadisha** – the voluntary agency of **Jews** who give their services freely to take care of the dead.
> 5 To show that everyone, rich or poor, is equal in death and is treated accordingly.

▶ BACKGROUND INFORMATION

Jewish tradition dictates that the utmost respect be shown for the dying and the dead person. As soon as someone has died their body is not to be left alone. Once death has been established the eyes and the lips are closed. The body is placed on the floor, covered with a sheet and a lighted candle is placed near to the head. Mirrors in the home are covered and any standing water is poured away. In the Jewish community it is considered to be a mitzvah (a good deed without any reward) to sit with a dead person and recite psalms. Although arrangements are made to carry out the burial as quickly as possible, burial is not permitted on **Shabbat**. The body is washed and prepared for burial before being carried, face-up, to the grave in a plain coffin. Adult males are buried in their prayer shawls (**tallit**).

The place of burial is marked after a short service during which each of the mourners shovels earth on to the coffin. A headstone is usually unveiled as soon as tradition allows; after 30 days in Israel and 11 months elsewhere.

▶ STARTING POINTS

Any discussion of death must be dealt with with great care and tact. At the same time it must be realised that death in all the great world religions is much more than the 'fact of life' that it can be in our sanitised Western culture. The rituals and ceremonies of death are intended to bring the worshipper in touch with death – and the life beyond.

1 If the children watch the news on television then they are likely to be familiar with the fact of death. Talk about deaths that have taken place recently – of the young and of the old. Talk about death as a universal experience. Discuss any instance in the news of young people, and children, having to face the reality of death. Why does this seem so 'unnatural'?
2 Discuss the way that the different religions try to prepare people for death. Why, for instance, should Jewish people be concerned to have their sins forgiven as they approach death? Why are people frightened of death? Introduce the idea of life after death.

▶ KEY WORDS

Chevra Kadisha; Jew; Moses; Scriptures; Shabbat; tallit.

▶ COPYMASTER

Copymaster 20 Death in a Jewish family

This copymaster reinforces understanding of the rituals surrounding the death of someone in the Jewish community. Cut out and match up the drawings with the captions. Write your own captions for those which do not have them.

JUDAISM

COPYMASTER 20

Name ....

DEATH IN A JEWISH FAMILY

As death draws near a person prays that God will let them recover.

Before a person dies they ask for everyone's forgiveness.

36

JUDAISM

MOURNING

> ► AIMS
> 1 To introduce the meaning of the word 'mourning'.
> 2 To introduce the idea of mourning the death of someone.
> 3 To show the gradual return to normal life after the initial period of mourning.
> 4 To emphasise the important part played by members of the Jewish community in helping someone to overcome bereavement.

► BACKGROUND INFORMATION

Jewish tradition lays down a clear framework of mourning for those who have lost someone close, and for the Jewish community as a whole. It applies to females over the age of 12 and males over 13 who have lost a parent, a spouse, a child or a brother or sister. The stages are:

Stage One
Between death and burial. The mourners are exempt from all positive **mitzvot** (wearing **tefillin**, praying, saying grace, etc.) for this short time. The mourner is not allowed to engage in any 'pleasurable' activities. Instead he or she must 'rend a garment'. Immediately the burial has taken place (usually within 24 hours of death) the close mourners go home and eat a meal of a hard-boiled egg and bread which is provided by someone else.

Stage Two
The seven days following burial is a time when normal obligations are suspended. Mourners cannot shave, bathe, go to work, use deodorants or perfume, have sexual relations, cut their hair or greet one another. Other members of the community visit them to offer their condolences. No public display of mourning, however, must take place during **Shabbat**.

Stage Three
Thirty days of lesser mourning then follow. During this time mourners may not shave, cut their hair, wear new clothes or attend any festive occasions.
In all, a person mourns for their parents for eleven months. Each day they recite the **Kaddish**. They light a candle on the anniversary of the person's death. The obligation to do so only ends with the death of the person themselves.

► STARTING POINTS

Again this topic, like the last one, needs to be dealt with with great tact and sympathy. At the same time understanding mourning is central to understanding the Jewish approach to death generally. In the Jewish community the main concern after someone dies is to help the close relatives who remain. Mourning is a disciplined attempt to help them to come to terms with their grief. Bearing this in mind, begin to explore the sense of loss that bereavement brings.
1 What do people miss most about those who have died?
2 How can mourning attempt to make this loss bearable?

► KEY WORDS

Kaddish; mitzvot; onan; Shabbat; shiva; synagogue; tefillin.

► COPYMASTER

Copymaster 21 Mourning
This sheet will reinforce understanding of the concept of mourning and in particular the structured form of mourning which happens in the Jewish community. Make drawings of the four aspects of mourning in a Jewish family which are illustrated. Describe what is happening in each situation.

✡ JUDAISM

COPYMASTER 21

Name ....

MOURNING

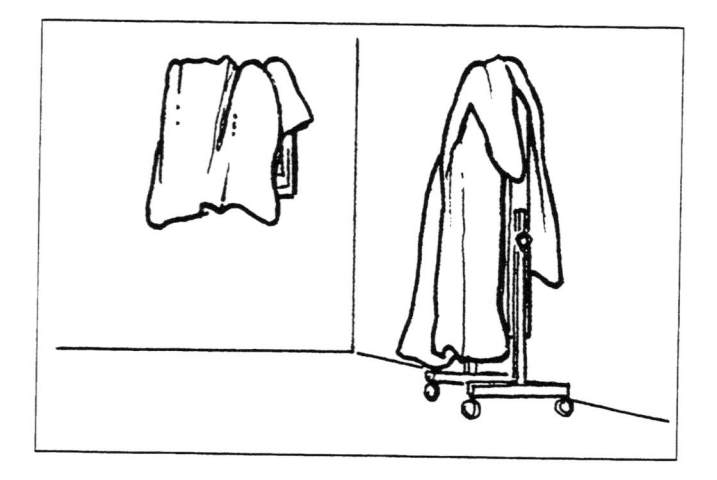

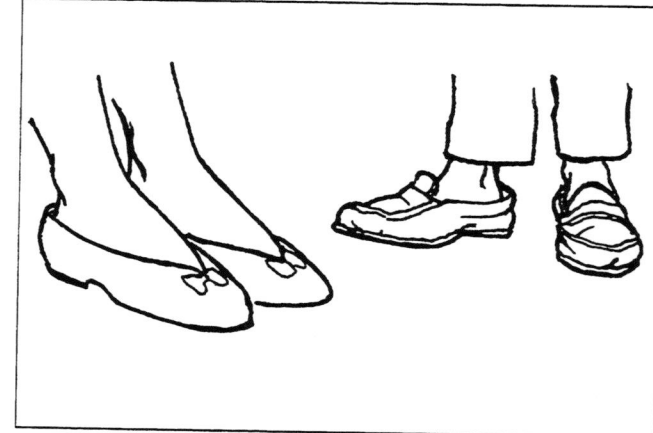

a _____

b _____

c _____

d _____

38

ISLAM

AROUND BIRTH

► AIMS
1. To introduce the **Adhan**.
2. To underline the importance of the first moments in a Muslim baby's life.
3. To describe the actions of Muslim parents when a baby is born.
4. To show the Muslim concern for the poor.
5. To introduce the start of a Muslim child's education with the **Bismillah** ceremony.

► BACKGROUND INFORMATION

At birth
As soon as a baby is born he or she is welcomed into the **ummah**; the worldwide family of Islam. The father whispers the call to prayer (the Adhan) into the baby's right ear and the command to rise up and worship **Allah** (the iqamah) in the left ear.
After the baby is taken home from hospital the tahneek ceremony is carried out by a highly respected, older member of the family. A small piece of a date, sugar or honey is placed in the baby's mouth. At the same time a **du'a** is said on the baby's behalf.

At seven days
A week after the baby's birth family and friends gather for the naming ceremony (**Aqiqah**). The baby is named by the father after passages from the **Qur'an** have been read out. The name will be derived either from one of Allah's 99 known names or from the name of **Muhammad**, Allah's Prophet. Male babies are also **circumcised** on this day – the same day on which Jews circumcise their male children.
The baby's head is shaved as a symbol that the child is rid of all misfortune. The child's hair is weighed and an equivalent amount in gold or silver given to the poor.

Bismillah
Takes place when the child is exactly four years, four months and four days old. It is a commemoration of the first occasion that the Angel **Jibril** appeared to Muhammad. It marks the beginning of the child's religious education which takes place in the **madressa**; 'the school at the **mosque**'.

► STARTING POINTS
1. Talk about the preparations that are made in a home for the arrival of a new baby. Then talk about the additional preparations made in a Muslim home. Look at a full version of the Adhan. Explain why Muslims want the first words spoken to a new-born baby to be that of Allah.
2. Talk about the significance that names can have. Why do many religions stress the importance of the choice of a baby's name? Link in the importance of the name of Allah or Muhammad in Muslim families. Also emphasize the importance of the Muslim community, the ummah.

► KEYWORDS
Adhan; Allah; Aqiqah; Bismillah; circumcision; du'a; Jibril; madressa; mosque; Muhammad; Qur'an; ummah.

► COPYMASTERS
Copymaster 22 What is happening?
This sheet reinforces understanding of the ritual surrounding the birth of a Muslim baby. Colour in each of the drawings. Explain what is happening on the sheet.
Copymaster 23 The Adhan
This copymaster gives more detail on the content of the Adhan itself. Answer questions on the Adhan.

☾ ISLAM   ☾ ✝ ✡ ☬

COPYMASTER 22   Name ....

WHAT IS HAPPENING?

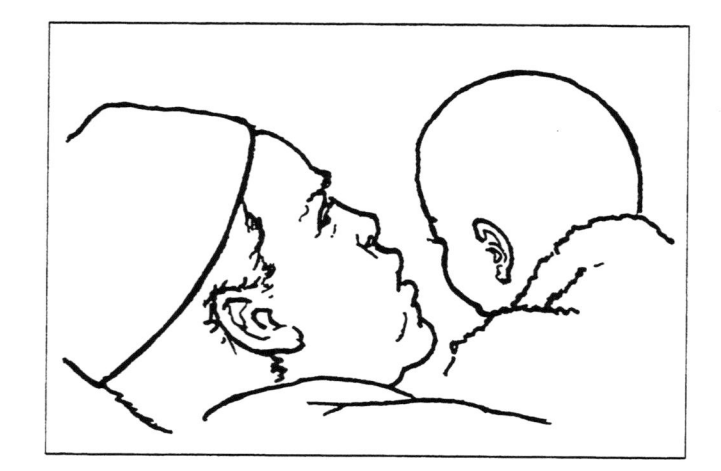

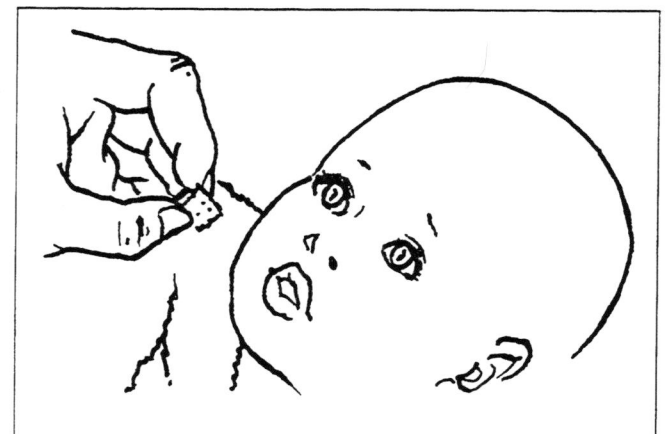

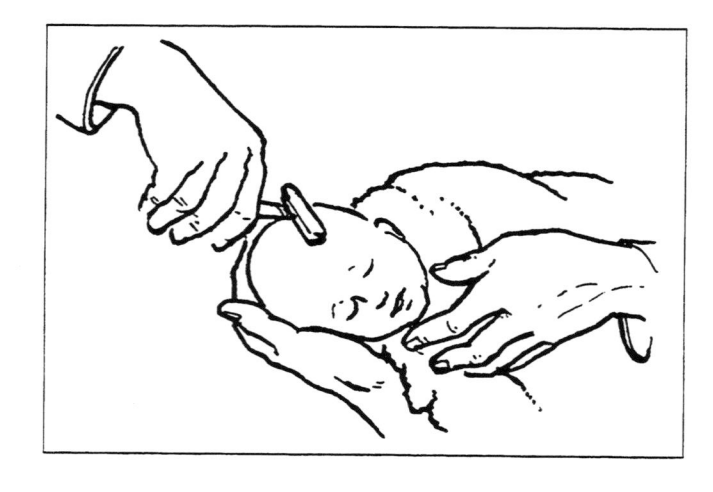

1 _____
_____
_____

2 _____
_____
_____

3 _____
_____
_____

4 _____
_____
_____

☬ ✡ † ☪ **ISLAM** ☾

COPYMASTER 23   Name ....

THE ADHAN

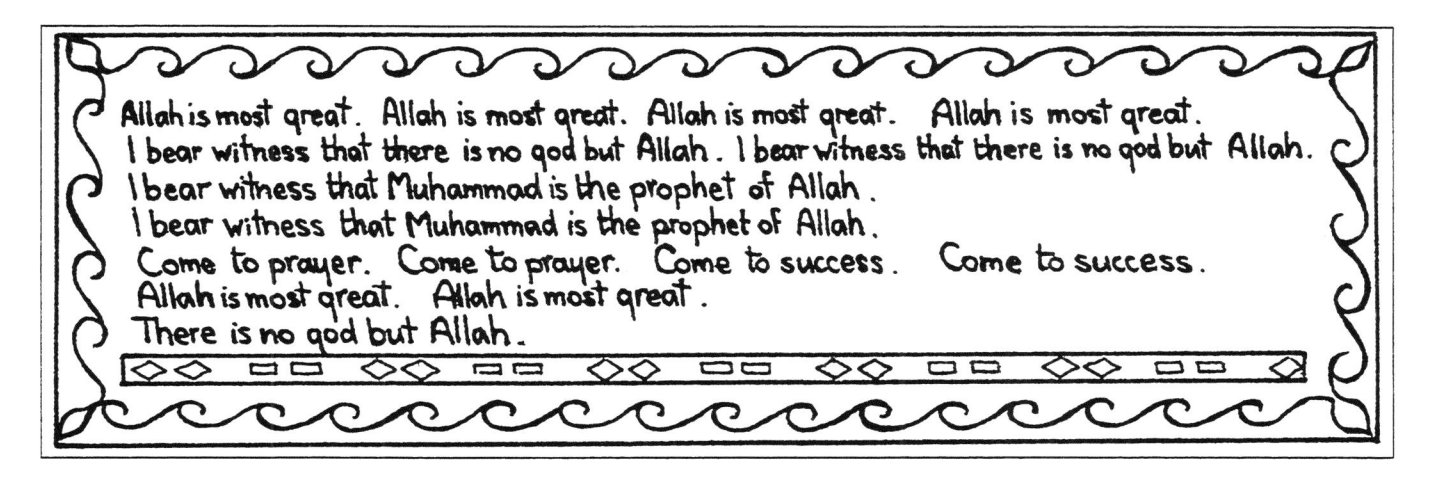

> Allah is most great. Allah is most great. Allah is most great. Allah is most great.
> I bear witness that there is no god but Allah. I bear witness that there is no god but Allah.
> I bear witness that Muhammad is the prophet of Allah.
> I bear witness that Muhammad is the prophet of Allah.
> Come to prayer. Come to prayer. Come to success. Come to success.
> Allah is most great. Allah is most great.
> There is no god but Allah.

1 According to the Muslim prayer, the Adhan, which is written out above:

   a What is the Muslim name for God? _____

   b Who is the prophet of Allah? _____

   c How many gods do Muslims believe in? _____

2 What is the name of the call that the mu'adhin is making from the top of the tower? _____

41

ISLAM

FAMILY LIFE

> ► AIMS
> 1 To show the importance attached to family life within the Muslim community.
> 2 To show the nature of the extended Muslim family.
> 3 To underline the pivotal role of the mother within the Muslim family.
> 4 To show the behaviour expected of children in a Muslim family.
> 5 To show the behaviour demanded of parents in a Muslim family.
> 6 To introduce the fact that grandparents are the head of any extended Muslim family.

► BACKGROUND INFORMATION

To Muslims the family unit is the basis of any healthy society and civilisation. This is because the institution of family life was introduced by **Allah** with the intention of providing a healthy and secure environment in which everyone, from the youngest to the oldest, can thrive and grow. Anything, therefore, which weakens the family in any way is dealt with strongly.

The family in question, however, is not the typical Western 'nuclear' family unit. That is made up of just two generations: parents and children. The Muslim family also includes grandparents, aunts and uncles, cousins and sometimes even neighbours and friends as well. A **hadith** makes the importance of the family for all Muslims very clear:

'Those who show the most perfect faith are those who possess the best disposition and are kindest to their families.'

The linchpin of every Muslim family is the mother. To be a good mother is the highest calling given to anyone in Islam. When a woman becomes a mother for the first time she takes on board an enormous responsibility. Not only must she provide her children with equal opportunities, but she must also ensure that they are given a secure and loving upbringing. They must be provided with the best possible education. Children, in return, also carry heavy responsibilities towards their parents. They must always show respect towards them and not argue with them. When their parents grow old the children must look after them. As a hadith says: 'May his nose be rubbed in the dust who found his parents approaching old age and did not enter Paradise by serving them.'

► STARTING POINTS

1 Ask questions about the children's family life. How many people live in their house? Do their grandparents live with them? Are their aunts, uncles and cousins nearby? Do they see much of their relatives? What are the differences between their family lives and those of most Muslims? What are the main advantages/disadvantages of having one's family close by, or even under the same roof?
2 Talk about the responsibilities of the children towards their parents and vice versa. Are they similar to those felt by a Muslim child?

► KEY WORDS

Allah; fast; hadith; Qur'an.

► COPYMASTER

Copymaster 24 Different families
This copymaster will help pupils to understand the difference in family culture between Western and traditional Muslim families. Draw a picture of a Western family when everyone is in the house at the same time. Draw a picture of a traditional Muslim family when everyone is in the house at the same time. List three differences between traditional Western and Muslim families.

ISLAM

COPYMASTER 24   Name ....

DIFFERENT FAMILIES

Differences:

1 _____
  _____
  _____

2 _____
  _____
  _____

3 _____
  _____
  _____

ISLAM

WOMEN

> ▶ AIMS
> 1 To outline the role played by women in Islam.
> 2 To explain the rules laid down in the **Qur'an** for the dress that women wear.
> 3 To outline the role that women play in worship.

▶ BACKGROUND INFORMATION

This is one of the most contentious areas in any debate about the role of Islam in the modern world. The Qur'an teaches that all men and women are the children of Adam and Eve (the first man and woman). This makes them equal in **Allah's** sight. God has, however, given them different roles to perform. Both the Qur'an and Muslim tradition have a great deal to say about this.

- From the time of **Muhammad**, Muslim women have had the right to own property in their own name.
- The Qur'an insists that all women should dress 'modestly' and behave decently in public. In many Muslim countries women wear the traditional long dress and head veil. Dressing in this way is called hijab.
- Women are permitted to attend the **mosque**, but they have their own separate washing facilities and prayer room. In this a distinction is made between men and women. Muslim men are expected to attend the mosque frequently and especially on Friday at midday. Women, though, are expected to always put the demands of their families first.

▶ STARTING POINTS

1 Muhammad told his followers: 'Modesty is part of the faith'. Talk about the meaning of modesty. How do Western people express it? What does it mean in a Muslim context?
2 Why are religious faith and modesty so closely bound up together?
3 Talk also about the different roles which men and women play in Islam.

▶ KEY WORDS

Allah; mosque; Muhammad; Qur'an.

▶ COPYMASTER

Copymaster 25 Women in Islam
This sheet begins to build a picture of how a woman is expected to behave in Muslim culture. Questions to be answered.

ISLAM

COPYMASTER 25

Name ....

WOMEN IN ISLAM

1 What does the Qur'an teach about how God looks on men and women? _____
_____

2 How does the Qur'an say women should dress? _____
_____
_____

3 Are women expected to pray in the mosque like men? _____
_____
_____

4 What is supposed to be more important than praying in the mosque for Muslim women? _____
_____

45

ISLAM

MARRIAGE

▶ AIMS

1. To introduce the idea of **arranged marriages**.
2. To introduce the **marriage contract**.
3. To describe the Muslim marriage ceremony.
4. To introduce the **dowry**.
5. To describe the celebrations which follow a wedding.

▶ BACKGROUND INFORMATION

Muslims are encouraged to marry, and the **Qur'an** allows men to have up to four wives, as long as each of the wives is treated equally. However, **polygamy** is only practised by a small number of people. Today it usually only happens if the first wife is unable to have children or is seriously ill. Even then it can only happen with her full consent.

Muslim tradition teaches that people can only be genuinely happy if they marry and have children. This is especially true for women. As one **hadith** puts it:

'Paradise lies at the feet of mothers.'

Two important points:

- As Muslim marriage is a life-long commitment (although divorce is allowed), great care is taken over the choice of a marriage partner. In most Muslim families parents and relations are involved in this choice.
- A Muslim wedding is essentially simple. The most important part is the signing of a **marriage contract** between the bridegroom and the bride's male guardian in front of two male Muslims. The contract lays down the amount of money to be included in the **mahr**, the money paid by the bridegroom's family to the bride. This remains the personal possession of the bride if the couple divorce.

▶ STARTING POINTS

1. Explain how an arranged marriage works. The role played by the families of both the man and the woman. Underline reasons why this is thought to be a good idea in Muslim communities. Speak of marriage as the bringing together of two families. How could the combined wisdom of two families make the choice of marriage partner more precise?
2. Talk about the advantages and disadvantages of this approach to marriage.

▶ KEYWORDS

Allah; arranged marriage; dowry; hadith; imam; mahr; marriage contract; mosque; polygamy; Qur'an.

▶ COPYMASTER

Copymaster 26 Choosing someone to marry

This sheet aims to bring some understanding of choosing someone to marry (whether your own or someone else's choice) and what sort of aspects might be taken into consideration. Fill in form to describe the sort of person you might like to marry. Discuss details on form with class.

ISLAM

COPYMASTER 26   Name ....

CHOOSING SOMEONE TO MARRY

1 Age – older than you/younger than you/same age?
   _____

2 Job – what would he or she do?
   _____

3 Personality – kind/thoughtful/lively/funny/quiet, etc.?
   _____

4 Interests or hobbies – sports/reading/music/films, etc.?
   _____

5 Hopes and ambitions – what would he or she want to do most in life?
   _____

6 Anything else important?
   _____

ISLAM

DEATH

▶ AIMS
1. To underline the importance of the **Adhan** throughout a Muslim's life, especially as life draws to a close.
2. To show the equality with which each Muslim is treated after death.
3. To describe the arrangements made by the Muslim community for the burial of those who have died.
4. To underline the importance of the body facing the holy city of **Makkah** as it is buried.

▶ BACKGROUND INFORMATION

It is reported that **Muhammad** prayed as he was dying:
'Allah, help me through the hardship and agony of death.'
He also asked for the forgiveness of his sins. Muslims try to follow the example of Muhammad as they approach their final hours. They believe strongly in the resurrection of the body and in a life after death, so they face the end of their lives with hope.

With death approaching, each Muslim hopes to be able to recite the **Shahadah** before dying. Relatives and friends around the bedside read passages from the **Qur'an**. They pray that **Allah** will be merciful to the person dying.

Then after death:

- The body is washed with scented water and dressed in white robes. A male is dressed in three robes and a woman in five.
- The body is taken to a **mosque** or to an open space. The funeral prayer includes the words: 'O God, pardon this dead person; lo, Thou are the most Forgiving, the most Merciful.'
- The body is taken to the cemetery to be buried; Muslims never **cremate** their dead. In Muslim countries a coffin is not used since Muslims believe that it is important for the body to be in direct contact with the earth. The body is placed with the right side facing **Makkah** and the head turned in the same direction.

▶ STARTING POINTS

1. Talk about the importance for Muslims of saying holy words at the beginning and ending of life. Talk also about the importance in Islam of stressing that all people are equal in death – since they are equal in God's sight. Stress the inequalities amongst people that there are in life; wealth, opportunities, food, etc. Why is death described as the 'great leveller'?
2. Discuss the two different points of view: that there is or isn't any form of life after death. Into which group do Muslims fit? What was the example set by Muhammad? How might a belief in life after death help someone to face up to dying?

▶ KEY WORDS

Adhan; Allah; cremation; Kaaba; Makkah; mosque; Muhammad; Qur'an; Shahadah.

▶ COPYMASTER

Copymaster 27 Facing up to death
This copymaster helps understanding of the importance to Muslims of their faith through critical points of their lives. Answer questions on sheet.

ISLAM

COPYMASTER 27   Name ....

FACING UP TO DEATH

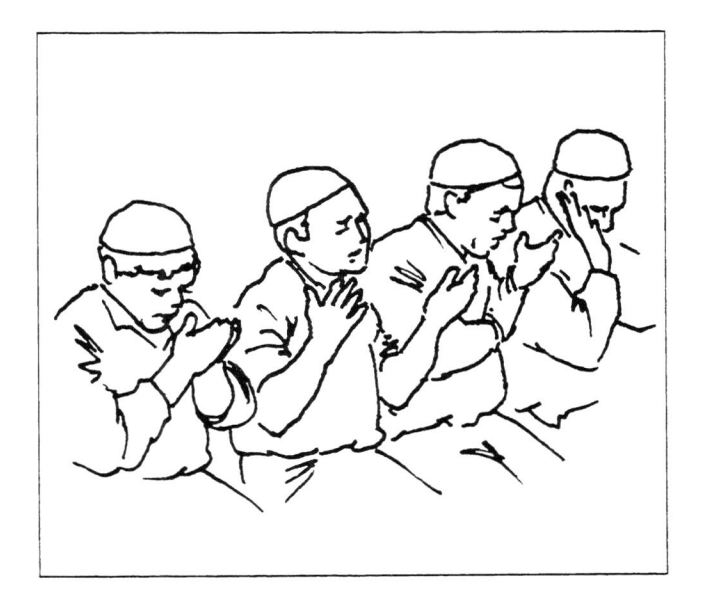

1 Which book is being read to the person who is dying?
_____

2 What does every Muslim hope to recite before they die?
_____

3 What are the friends of the person who is dying doing?
_____

4 During their lifetimes Muslims will hear or say the Adhan at two special times. When are these two special times?

   a _____

   b _____

5 At what other times will they hear the Adhan said?
_____

49

SIKHISM

NAME-GIVING

► AIMS

1 To introduce the children to the Sikh naming ceremony.
2 To emphasise the special role played by the **Guru Granth Sahib** in this as in other Sikh ceremonies.
3 To show that the drinking of **amrit** and the eating of **karah parshad** are important elements in the Sikh name-giving ceremony.

► BACKGROUND INFORMATION

Each of the religions in this series looks upon the creation of new life as one of the most important activities of God. Sikhism is no exception. As **Guru** Arjan made clear when he was speaking of the birth of his only son, Hargobind:
'The True Guru (God) has sent the child.'
This reflects a verse which Guru Arjan's mother composed when her son was born. She speaks about the future and says:
'Dear Son, this is your mother's blessing. May God never be out of your mind even for a moment. Meditation of God should be your constant concern . . . May you love the company of God's people. May God robe you with honour and may your food be the singing of God's praises.'
This is the prayer of all Sikh parents for their children.

Name-Giving
The name-giving ceremony is the first act in the solemn responsibility of the parents to bring their children up in the Sikh faith. A tiny amount of amrit (holy water) is placed on the tip of a sword – and the baby's lips are touched with it. (Amrit is a mixture of sugar and water, and is used in Sikh worship on particularly special occasions.) The baby is also presented with a **kara** – a steel bracelet which symbolises the eternal nature of God, with no beginning or end, and the unity to be found in the Sikh community. The kara is worn at all times on the right wrist.
The parents of boys have two further responsibilities:
- They must make sure that their son does not have his hair cut. To a Sikh long hair is a symbol of dedication to God.
- As soon as their son is old enough to tie it for himself he must wear a **turban**.

The child's name is chosen by opening the pages of the holy book, the Guru Granth Sahib, at random. The child's name will begin with the first letter of the first word at the top of the right-hand page. Many Sikh names can be either male or female, so to distinguish them a further word is added to the end of the name. For boys the word is Singh – meaning lion; for girls it is Kaur – meaning princess. The naming service is ended, as every Sikh service is ended, with the sharing of karah parshad – a mix of flour, butter, sugar and water. The sharing of karah parshad symbolizes the unity of all people.

► STARTING POINTS

1 Talk about names. What would life be like if we didn't have a name? What problems would that cause? What do our names say about us – do they have a meaning? If so, do we know what that meaning is? Do we live up to our name?
2 The Sikh naming ceremony. Why do Sikhs use the Guru Granth Sahib to help them in naming their children? Why do Sikhs believe that God should be involved in a choice of a name? What difference might this make to the baby in the future? How are males and females distinguished in the Sikh community?

► KEY WORDS

Amrit; granthi; gurdwara; Guru Granth Sahib; kara; karah parshad; kirpan; turban.

SIKHISM

► COPYMASTERS

Copymaster 28 Names

This sheet highlights the importance of names and their possible significance. See of you can find out if your own name has a special meaning. Write the meaning on the sheet. List six favourite names. Why are they your favourite names? Say what your own choice of name would have been for yourself and why you would have chosen it.

Copymaster 29 Name graph

This copymaster will aid understanding of the popularity of various names, and why they have been chosen. Carry out a survey to find out the most popular names in your class. Enter the findings on a grid. Answer questions on sheet.

Copymaster 30 The Sikh name-giving ceremony

This copymaster will reinforce understanding of the ritual of the Sikh name-giving ceremony. Describe what is happening in each of the drawings. Draw and describe one aspect of the ceremony not illustrated. Colour all the drawings.

SIKHISM

COPYMASTER 28

Name ....

NAMES

Does your name have a special meaning? If so, what is it?

_____

_____

What are your favourite names?

_____

_____

Explain why they are your favourite names.

     NAME   WHY ?

1 _____

2 _____

3 _____

4 _____

5 _____

6 _____

If I could have chosen my own name it would have been

_____ because _____

_____

SIKHISM

COPYMASTER 29

Name ....

NAME GRAPH

Name

1

2

3

4

5

6

7

8

9

10

         1   2   3   4   5

Number of people in my class with this name

Three of these names mean:

1 Name _____

Meaning _____

2 Name _____

Meaning _____

3 Name _____

Meaning _____

SIKHISM

COPYMASTER 30

Name ....

THE SIKH NAME-GIVING CEREMONY

1

2

3

4

54

SIKHISM

SERVING OTHERS

> ► AIMS
> 1 To show the meaning and importance in Sikhism of **sewa**.
> 2 To underline the important emphasis that is laid on serving others in the Sikh community.
> 3 To tell the story of Bhal Khanaya.

► BACKGROUND INFORMATION

Practising Sikhs are expected to devote their energies to a lifetime of serving others. By serving others they are, in effect, serving their great spiritual teachers, the **Gurus**, and God. In practice, this service will be directed mainly towards the Sikh community. However, as the story of Bhal Khanaya makes clear (see Pupils' Book), it should not be confined to one's own community. God is pleased with service which is offered to the whole human race.

Serving the community is an art which every Sikh needs to learn, and the **gurdwara** is the best place in which this can happen. Within any community of Sikh believers:
- the gurdwara needs to be repaired and cleaned.
- the needs of the worshipping congregation need to be met.
- the shoes of those worshipping in the gurdwara need to be looked after.
- food needs to be prepared and served in the **langar**.

The langar is a very important part of Sikh life (see also next unit) because it accomplishes two basic functions. It provides the means for one Sikh to serve another and it overcomes any caste divisions. In the langar all people, from whatever caste, are equal. The langar also provides the means by which the poor can be fed.

Sewa (the serving of others) leads to many small acts of kindness but it also encourages Sikhs to commit themselves to much larger acts of kindness. **Guru Nanak** was particularly concerned with people suffering from leprosy, and established his own hospital for them. Sikhs have established countless hospitals and schools because of the teaching of sewa.

► STARTING POINTS

1 Encourage the children to think about the importance of serving others. How does it take place within the home? How does it take place within the school? How does it take place within society generally? What is the main motivation behind the teaching of Sikhism on serving others?
2 Provide the opportunity for the children to work out ways in which they could serve others. Divide the considerations into help provided within the home and help given at school to others. Talk about ways in which the needs of others can be identified.

► KEY WORDS

Gurdwara; Guru; Guru Gobind Singh; Guru Nanak; langar; sewa.

► COPYMASTER

Copymaster 31 Helping other people
This sheet reinforces the idea of helping others and the importance placed on this in the Sikh community. Colour each of the drawings. Write underneath each drawing what the person is doing to help others.

SIKHISM

COPYMASTER 31

Name ....

HELPING OTHER PEOPLE

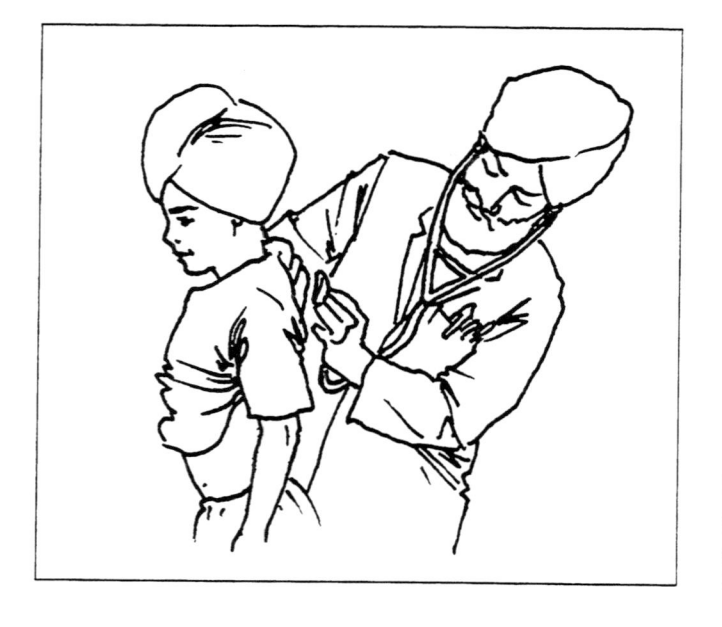

_____
_____
_____

_____
_____
_____

Can you help other people if you do not belong to a religion?

56

SIKHISM

SHARING WITH OTHERS

> ► AIMS
> 1 To introduce the **langar** – an essential part of every **gurdwara**.
> 2 To introduce the notion of sharing with others which stands at the heart of Sikhism.
> 3 To link the idea of sharing with others with the meal in the langar at the end of the service.
> 4 To link the langar with the examples of **Guru Nanak** and Guru Amar Das.
> 5 To introduce the notion of the equality of all as practised in the langar.

► BACKGROUND INFORMATION

The langar meal is eaten at the end of every Sikh act of worship and it is an integral part of that worship. It is not merely a social event. It symbolizes two important aspects of Sikh belief:
- The providential care of God who takes care of all the material needs of his followers.
- The openness of Sikhs to all men and women, whether they are Sikh believers or not. Anyone in the congregation, and outside, can receive this example of Sikh hospitality and Sikhs would be offended if it were refused.

Within the context of worship **karah parshad** and the langar act as open declarations that God's love is available to all and no one has the right to deny it. This equality is stressed by the fact that within the **diwan** and the langar both men and women work together in total equality. Just as women are not banned from any spiritual activity in the gurdwara so men have the opportunity of learning to share and serve others in the langar.

► STARTING POINTS

1 Explain to the class that the langar is an open kitchen at the gurdwara where everyone is welcome to share in the meal after an act of worship. If possible, visit a local gurdwara to see the diwan and the langar. Talk about the kind of food provided in the langar. Discuss why it is **vegetarian**. Plan such a meal with the children.
2 Talk to the children about sharing. What do they already share with others; clothes, toys, etc.? Are there any items that they would not be prepared to share? How about giving personal possesssions away to those in need? Why is sharing such an important belief at the heart of Sikhism?

► KEY WORDS

Diwan; gurdwara; Guru Nanak; karah parshad; langar; vegetarian.

► COPYMASTER

Copymaster 32 Sharing in a gurdwara
This copymaster reinforces the nature of the work which is involved in bringing a langar meal together and how this basic work is something that must be done by everyone in the Sikh community. Put the jobs in the right order. Colour the drawings. Draw a picture of yourself doing one of these jobs.

SIKHISM

COPYMASTER 32   Name ....

SHARING IN A GURDWARA

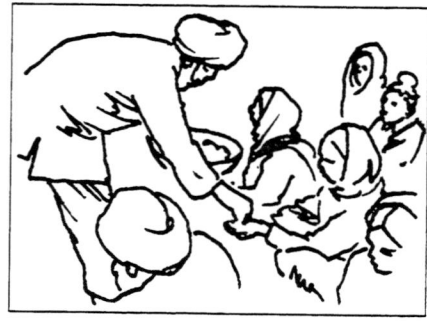

ORDER OF JOBS:

1 _____
2 _____
3 _____
4 _____
5 _____
6 _____

58

SIKHISM

WEARING THE TURBAN

▶ AIMS
1 To introduce the meaning and the value that long hair has for a Sikh.
2 To underline the obligation on every Sikh to look after their hair properly.
3 To show how Sikh children are taught to look after their hair.
4 To introduce the **turban**.

▶ BACKGROUND INFORMATION

Wearing a turban has become almost synonymous with being a Sikh in the minds of most observers. During the 1950s and the 1960s, as the Sikh community in this country was growing, the wearing of the turban often caused friction in the work place and with governing authorities. It was some time, for instance, before Sikhs were allowed to wear turbans instead of crash helmets on their motor-cycles.

There are many reasons why wearing a turban is synonymous with being a Sikh for a man.

- Pictures of the **Gurus** always show them wearing turbans. They commanded all Sikh believers to imitate them as closely as possible. As the **Adi Granth** says: 'The Guru and the **disciple** are one' (444). The Gurus also taught that their hair is a special gift from God, and that it should not be cut. In men long hair is seen as a sign of strength, and in women a sign of great beauty.
- The turban acts as a kind of 'uniform'. In the beginning the Gurus wanted a form of clothing which clearly marked out Sikhs from non-Sikhs. The turban fitted that bill.
- The symbolism behind the turban is its most important quality to a Sikh. Although a turban does help a Sikh man to keep his hair tidy, that is not the main reason for wearing it. This can be seen when lengths of cloth are exchanged at a wedding ceremony, or when the head of a family has died. When the person ties a turban with a new length of cloth, the people know that power and authority within a family, or within a community, has passed from one person to another.

▶ STARTING POINTS
1 Talk about hair and the important role that it has played in religious ideas. An example is the Old Testament character of Samson. Why has long hair so often been associated with strength? Why should long hair in a woman be linked with beauty? Why do Sikhs see it as their religious responsibility not to cut their hair?
2 If possible invite a Sikh into the class to show pupils how the turban is put together. Compare the turban with the head-coverings which Sikh boys wear.

▶ KEY WORDS
Adi Granth; disciple; Guru; kangha; patka; turban.

▶ COPYMASTER
Copymaster 33 Tying a turban
This worksheet will give an idea of the complexity of tying a turban, and therefore the lengths that a Sikh man goes to on a regular basis to keep to the ideals of his religion. Cut out each of the drawings. Paste the drawings into your exercise book in the correct order. Line up the descriptions to match each of the drawings. Put the descriptions alongside the drawings in your own words.

SIKHISM

COPYMASTER 33

Name ....

TYING A TURBAN

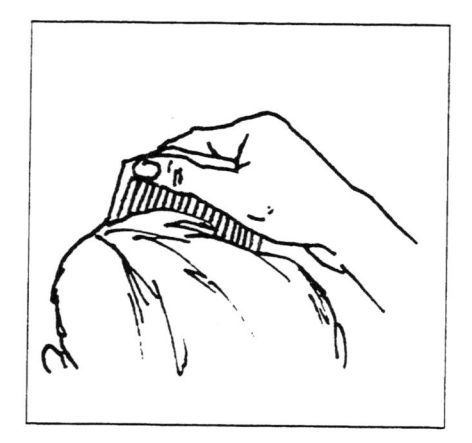

1 The hair is tied and then plaited.

2 The cloth is being wound around the head with one end held between the teeth.

3 The hair is fixed in place using a kangha.

4 The turban is tied completely in place.

5 The last piece of cloth is tucked in.

6 The turban is straightened on the head.

SIKHISM

THE AMRIT CEREMONY

> ► AIMS
> 1 To introduce the **Amrit** ceremony.
> 2 To introduce the **Khalsa**.
> 3 To draw attention to the background of the initiation ceremony.
> 4 To show the importance of amrit (nectar) in the ceremony.
> 5 To list the rules to which all members of the Khalsa commit themselves.

► BACKGROUND INFORMATION

- The Amrit ceremony (**Amrit Pahul**) can take place at any time in the adult life of a Sikh and marks a new level of commitment from them. Many Sikhs do not enter into this commitment. They are known as **Sahaj-Dhari** which means that they are seeking God. Other Sikhs keep some of the rules of the Khalsa and do not cut their hair, although they have not been baptised with amrit or gone through the Amrit Pahul ceremony. These people are known as **Kesh-Dhari**.
- The service is carried out and witnessed by five Sikhs who already belong to the Khalsa. These people symbolise the five followers (**Panj Pyares**) who were willing to lay down their lives for **Guru Gobind Singh**. The original Panj Pyares were Sikhs chosen by Guru Gobind Singh because of their willingness to follow him even to the point of death. They mix sugar with water to make amrit (nectar). This mixture is drunk by each of the candidates and they are also anointed with it. The anointing with amrit is the Sikh baptism.
- Each of the candidates promises to wear all the **Five Ks** (kesh – uncut hair, **kangha** – comb, **kirpan** – special sword, **kara** – steel bangle, kachs – traditional shorts), to recite their daily prayers, not to use tobacco or drugs, to abstain from alcohol, not to commit adultery and not to eat meat which has already been killed for religious purposes.
- Being a member of the Khalsa shows the commitment of the individual to their faith, and symbolises their willingness to fight, if necessary, to defend their faith.

► STARTING POINTS

1 Ask the children to draw up their own rules for a society. How do their rules compare with those demanded by the Khalsa? Why are such rules necessary? What is really being asked of those who join? What is commitment? What do the members of the Khalsa commit themselves to?
2 Talk about the transition from childhood to adulthood. What are the main differences between the two? When is one left behind and the other reached? How do other religions mark this transition? Why are ceremonies around this time important? What are they really marking?

► KEY WORDS

Amrit; Amrit Pahul; Five Ks; Guru Gobind Singh; Guru Granth Sahib; kangha; kara; Kesh-Dhari; Khalsa; kirpan; Panj Pyares; Sahaj-Dhari.

► COPYMASTER

Copymaster 34 The Sikh Amrit ceremony.
This copymaster will reinforce understanding of the Amrit ceremony which is a very special time for those initiated into the Khalsa. Look at the drawings of the Sikh Amrit ceremony. Colour in each picture. Explain what is happening in each drawing.

SIKHISM

COPYMASTER 34

Name ....

THE SIKH AMRIT CEREMONY

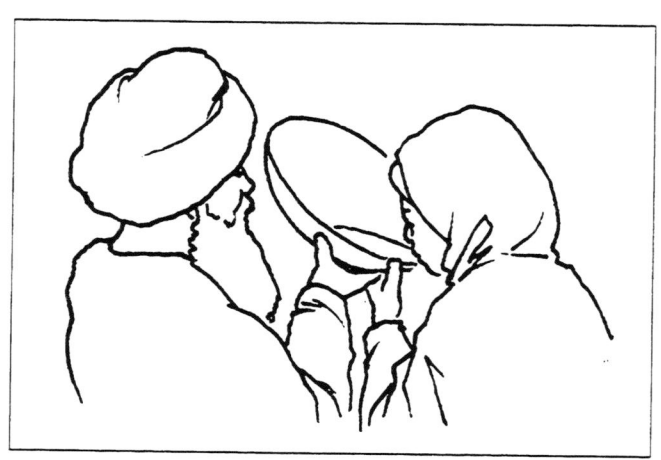

What is happening?

1 _____

_____

2 _____

_____

_____

3 _____

_____

_____

4 _____

_____

_____

SIKHISM

MARRIAGE

> ► AIMS
> 1 To introduce the Sikh marriage ceremony as the **Anand Karaj**, the ceremony of bliss.
> 2 To underline the importance of the **Guru Granth Sahib** for this as for all Sikh ceremonies.
> 3 To introduce the notion of 'arranged marriages'.
> 4 To show the importance of the couple walking past the Guru Granth Sahib several times bowing as they go.

► BACKGROUND INFORMATION

In the Sikh community marriage is not simply a matter which involves two people alone. Through marriage two whole families become intertwined. For this reason the bride and the groom have to be acceptable to both families. The basic conditions that have to be met before marriage are that the bride and groom must:
- Both be believing Sikhs.
- Have already met and be willing to accept each other as partners for life. They must enter into marriage freely and willingly.

Anand Karaj, the ceremony of bliss.
- Although it does not matter where a Sikh wedding ceremony is held, as long as the Guru Granth Sahib is present, in Britain the ceremony invariably takes place in the **gurdwara**. The bride and groom indicate that they are entering into marriage freely by bowing in front of the holy book.
- As the couple walk clockwise around the Guru Granth Sahib flower-petals are thrown over them. These symbolise the fragrance of the new life that they will now share together.

► STARTING POINTS

1 Talk about the different ways in which people meet each other in this country: at a dance, at a club, through friends, through church, at a youth-club. Explain what happens in an 'arranged marriage'. Why are Sikh, and other, marriages 'arranged'? Talk about the advantages and disadvantages of the system.
2 Talk about the use of symbolism in Sikh and other weddings, e.g. marriage and the giving of a ring, the dominance of the colour red, the tying together of the bride and groom, etc.

► KEY WORDS

Anand Karaj; gurdwara; Guru Granth Sahib; karah parshad; shalwar-kameez; turban.

► COPYMASTER

Copymaster 35 A Sikh wedding
This worksheet will reinforce understanding of the Sikh wedding ceremony. Cut out each of the drawings. Stick them into your exercise book in the correct order. Write two sentences describing what is happening in each drawing. Colour in each drawing.

SIKHISM

COPYMASTER 35   Name ....

A SIKH WEDDING

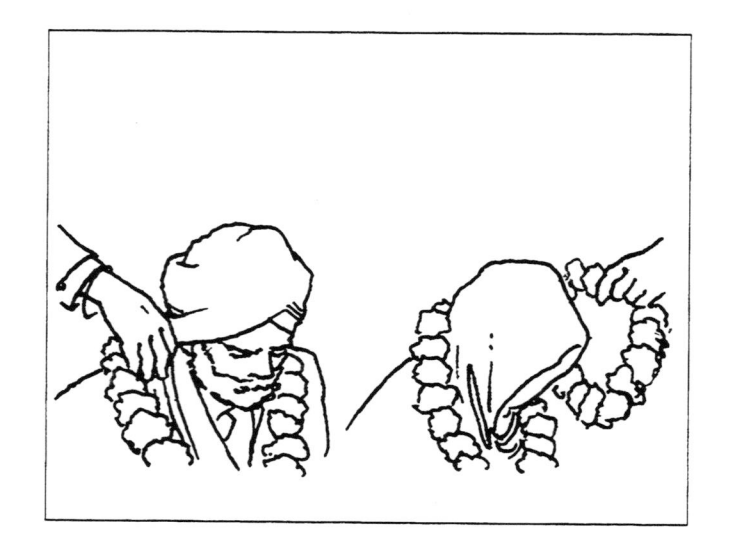

SIKHISM

DEATH

> ► AIMS
> 1 To introduce the way that Sikhs try to approach death.
> 2 To underline the part played by the **Guru Granth Sahib** in the final hours of a person's life.
> 3 To draw attention to the fact that Sikhs always **cremate** their dead.
> 4 To introduce the **Akhand Path**; the continual reading of the **Adi Granth**.

► BACKGROUND INFORMATION

When facing death a Sikh is comforted by readings from the Holy **Scriptures**. A favourite passage, often read in the last hours of a person's life, is Guru Arjan's 'Hymn of Peace'.

It would be nonsense to suggest that a Sikh does not feel death as acutely as anyone else. Great sadness is felt on the death of a loved one. However, it is hope, rather than sadness, which characterises the death of a Sikh. Death removes the last barrier that exists between God and the believer.

In the **Punjab**, the home of Sikhism, a funeral pyre is traditionally lit under the body by the eldest son. The evening hymn, the **Sohilla**, is sung at the same time. This expresses how each Sikh believer feels about death, and life after death. It says that:

- Every person possesses in themselves a part of God which will eventually return to God.
- The soul can never die.
- Through a combination of good works and acts of religious devotion the soul will eventually be reunited to God, although it may need to be reborn many times before this union takes place. Sikhs believe strongly in **reincarnation**.

A continual reading of the whole Adi Granth which is the shorter version of the Sikh holy book can take place following death. This reading is known as the Akhand Path and takes around 48 hours to complete. If this is arranged all the adult relatives of the dead person take part. Sikhs set aside a specific time for mourning.

► STARTING POINTS

1 Talk about death. What is death?
2 How can anything survive death? What might the soul be? Explore with the children the idea that human beings could possess something which goes beyond the body. Talk about the capacity of humans to love, feel deeply, grieve, feel sad, etc. Talk about whether these capacities could belong to a 'spiritual' dimension to our beings.

► KEY WORDS

Adi Granth; Akhand Path; cremation; Five Ks; gurdwara; Guru Granth Sahib; Punjab; reincarnation; Scriptures; Sohilla.

► COPYMASTER

Copymaster 36 A Sikh funeral
This copymaster will aid understanding of the Sikh approach to death and the involvement of religious ritual at this time. Answer questions printed on the sheet. Identify four objects drawn as part of the Sikh approach to death. Write one sentence of explanation underneath each drawing.

SIKHISM

COPYMASTER 36   Name ....

A SIKH FUNERAL

1 What does each Sikh try to say as death draws near?

2 What does the word mean?

3 After someone's death a special event may take place. What is it called? What do the relatives do as part of this event?

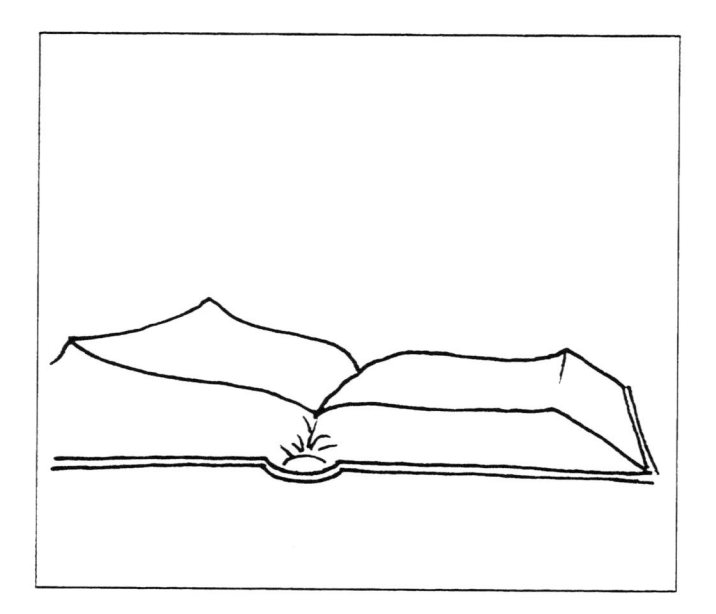

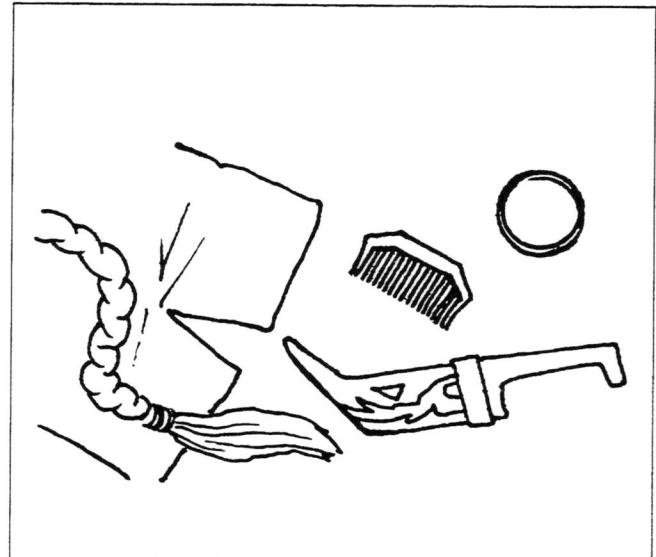

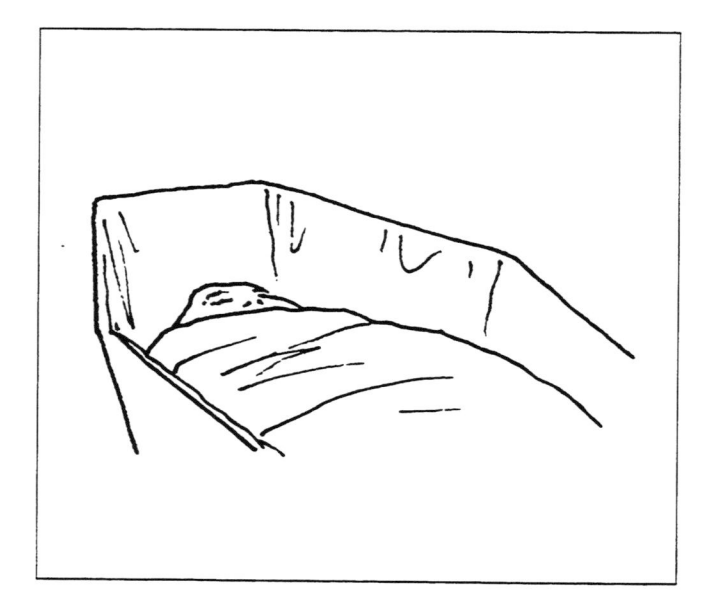

66

PUPILS' GLOSSARY

Abraham: The first person in the Bible to believe in one God.
Adhan: The Call to Prayer made five times a day to Muslims from a mosque.
Adi Granth: The shorter version of the holy book of the Sikh religion.
Advent: The time of the year when some Christians prepare for the coming of Jesus.
Allah: The Muslim name for God.
Altar: The place at the front of the church where the most important parts of the service are conducted.
Amrit: The holy food eaten by Sikhs in their services.
Amrit Pahul: The service at which Sikhs join the Khalsa.
Amritsar: The Sikh holy city in the Punjab in India.
Anand Karaj: The Sikh wedding service called the 'ceremony of bliss'.
Angel: A messenger sent by God to human beings.
Angel Gabriel (Jibril): The angel who appeared to Mary and also to Muhammad.
Archbishop of Canterbury: The leader of the Church of England.
Ark: The place in the synagogue where the important scrolls are kept.
Ash Wednesday: The day which begins the fast of Lent in the Christian Church.

Baptism: A symbolic service for entering the Christian Church involving dipping in water or sprinkling with water.
Baptist Church: A Protestant Church which baptises adults and not children.
Barmitzvah: Ceremony which marks a Jewish boy becoming an adult.
Batmitzvah: Ceremony to mark a Jewish girl becoming an adult.
Bethlehem: The village in Palestine in which Jesus was born.
Bible: The holy book of Christians.
Bishop: An important priest in the Church of England or Roman Catholic Church.
Bismillah: The ceremony at which Muslim children learn the first words from the Qur'an, which mean 'in the name of God, the merciful, the compassionate'.
Black Stone: The stone given by Allah to Ibrahim, which is part of the Kaaba.

Cardinal: One of the most important priests in the Roman Catholic Church.
Cathedral: The main church in an area where the Bishop takes the services.
Chapel: Small place of worship belonging to a Free Church.
Chauri: Fan which is waved over the Guru Granth Sahib.
Chevra Kadisha: Jewish group of volunteers who help with dying people and the funeral.
Christening: An alternative name for the baptism of a baby.
Christian: A person who follows the teachings of Jesus and usually belongs to a church.
Christmas: The festival, on 25th December, when Christians remember the birth of Jesus.
Church: The building in which Christians worship God.
Church of England: The main Christian Church in England.
Circumcision: Jewish and Muslim ceremony to remove the foreskin of a boy's penis.
Citadel: A Salvation Army place of worship.
Confessional: The place in Roman Catholic and some Church of England churches where people confess their sins to a priest.
Confirmation: The service in the Church of England or Roman Catholic Church which makes people full members of their church.
Cremation: The burning of dead bodies, the alternative to burial.
Crib: The model made at Christmas time to show the birth of Jesus in a stable.
Crucifix: Statue in a church which shows Jesus on the cross.

PUPILS' GLOSSARY

David: The most loved king in Israel's history.
Denominations: The different Christian Churches.
Devil: The evil force which opposes God and tempts human beings.
Disciple: Someone who follows the teachings of a religious leader.
Diwan: The main act of worship in a Sikh gurdwara.
Dowry: Gift given by a bridegroom to his bride in Islam and Sikhism.

Easter The most important festival in the Christian Church when people remember the death of Jesus and his return to life.
Exodus: The journey of the Israelites out of slavery in Egypt.

Fast: Going without food or drink for religious reasons.
Five Ks: Five things beginning with the letter K which are symbols of membership of the Sikh Khalsa.
Five Pillars: The most important beliefs of Muslims.
Font: The container in a church in which water is kept for baptism.
Free Churches: The Christian Churches which do not belong to the Church of England, Roman Catholic or Orthodox Churches.

Godparent: A person who promises a baby when it is baptised that he or she will look after him or her.
Golden Temple: The holiest place in the Sikh religion, which is in Amritsar.
Good Friday: The day of the year in the Christian Church when Christians remember the death of Jesus.

Granthi: The official in a gurdwara who looks after the Guru Granth Sahib.
Gurdwara: A Sikh place of worship.
Guru: A Sikh holy teacher and leader.
Guru Gobind Singh: The last of the ten Sikh Gurus.
Guru Granth Sahib: The fullest version of the Sikh holy book.
Guru Nanak: The first Sikh Guru and the founder of the religion.

Hajj: The pilgrimage which Muslims take to Makkah.
Hajji: A man or a woman who has been on the Hajj.
Halo: The circle around someone's head in a painting to show that they are very holy.
Heaven: The place where religious people believe God lives, which they hope to reach after they die.
Hebrew: The Jewish language.
Hegira: The journey that Muhammad took with his followers in 622. They travelled from Makkah to Madinah.
High Priest: The most important Jewish leader at the time of Jesus.
Holy Communion: The sharing of bread and wine to remember Jesus in Christian churches.
Holy Spirit: God's spirit, which Christians believe is given to people on earth to help them.
Huppah: A Jewish wedding canopy.
Hymn: A song which people sing together in a church or a gurdwara.

Ibrahim: The Muslim name for Abraham.
Icon: A religious painting of a saint or Jesus used by Orthodox Christians in worship.
Iconostasis: A screen at the front of an Orthodox church.
Imam: The leader of prayers in a mosque.
Incense: A substance which is burnt to make a sweet-smelling smoke in many religious services.
Islam: The religion which Muhammad passed on from Allah to the people.
Israel: A country where Jews live.

PUPILS' GLOSSARY

Jerusalem: The capital city of Israel.
Jesus: The person Christians believe to be the Son of God and the founder of Christianity.
John the Baptist: The prophet who prepared the people for the coming of Jesus.
Joseph: The husband of Mary and the father of Jesus.

Kaaba: The Muslim shrine at the centre of Makkah.
Kachs: The shorts worn by Sikhs to show that they are ready for battle.
Kaddish: A Jewish prayer which praises God.
Kangha: A comb used by Sikhs, one of the Five Ks.
Kara: The bracelet which Sikhs wear to remind them of God.
Karah Parshad: Food shared by all Sikhs at the end of a service.
Kesh: The uncut hair of Sikhs.
Ketubah: The marriage document given to a Jewish bride before she marries.
Khadijah: The wife of Muhammed and his first disciple.
Khalsa: The Sikh brotherhood of believers.
Kirpan: A short knife which is one of the Five Ks in Shikism.
Kirtan Sohilla: A Sikh prayer.
Kosher: The food which Jews are allowed to eat.

Langar: The kitchen in a Sikh gurdwara where everyone can eat.
Lent: The time before Easter when some Christians fast.

Madinah: The town in which Muhammad spent much of his life.
Makkah: The holiest city in Islam.
Marriage contract: The document given to a Muslim bride by her husband.
Mary: The mother of Jesus, highly respected by many Christians.
Mass: The main service in a Roman Catholic church.
Maundy Thursday: The day on which Christians remember Jesus washing the feet of his disciples.
Methodist Church: A leading Free Church set up by John Wesley.
Mezuzah: Small box which contains the Shema.
Mihrab: Hole in the wall of a mosque which shows worshippers which way to pray.
Minaret: The tower of a mosque from which the Call to Prayer is given.
Minister: The word used for a priest in a Free Church.
Mohel: A man who circumcises Jewish boys.
Moses: The early Jewish leader who led the Jews out of slavery in Egypt and taught them many of God's laws.
Mosque: A Muslim place of prayer.
Mu'adhin: The man who calls Muslims to prayer from the top of the minaret.
Muhammad: The Prophet of Allah whose teachings form the foundation of Islam.
Muslim: A person who worships Allah.

Nazareth: The village in which Jesus grew up.

Old Testament: The first part of the Christian Bible, which also makes up the Jewish Bible.
Onan: The name given to Jewish mourners before their relative who has died is buried.
Orthodox Church: The main Christian Church in countries in Eastern Europe and the Mediterranean.

Palestine: The country in which Jesus lived.
Palm Sunday: The day on which Christians remember Jesus entering Jerusalem on a donkey.
Panj Pyares: The five Sikhs who conduct the Amrit Pahul ceremony.

PUPILS' GLOSSARY

Parable: A special story told by Jesus. It taught the people about God.
Passover: A Jewish festival. The Passover reminds Jews of the journey from slavery in Egypt.
Pastor: The leader of a Baptist church.
Patka: Head covering for a Sikh boy.
Pesach: The most important Jewish festival of the year.
Peter, Saint: One of the disciples of Jesus who became the first Bishop of Rome.
Pilgrim: A man or a woman who travels to a holy place, usually on foot.
Pilgrimage: Any journey taken to a holy place, such as Makkah.
Pontius Pilate: The Roman governor of Palestine who put Jesus to death.
Pope: The leader of the Roman Catholic Church.
Prayer book: The book which contains the services in a church or a synagogue.
Prayer Hall: The main hall in a mosque where prayers take place.
Prayer-mat: A mat which is laid out and pointed towards Makkah, the holy city. Muslims kneel on it to pray.
Priest: The word for a leader in many Christian churches.
Punjab: The country in North India where Sikhism began.
Prophet: A man or a woman sent by God with a message for the people.
Psalm: A holy song from the Jewish Scriptures.
Pulpit: The raised platform from which the sermon is given.

Quakers: Members of a Free Church known as the Religious Society of Friends.
Qur'an: The holy book of Muslims.

Rabbi: The leader of a Jewish synagogue.
Rak'ah: A series of movements which a Muslim does when he or she is praying.
Ramadan: The most important month in the Muslim year when a Muslim goes without food during each day.
Registry Office: The place in which many people who do not wish to marry in a church get married.
Roman Catholic Church: The largest and oldest Christian Church.
Rosary: A set of beads which many Christians, especially Roman Catholics, use to help them to pray.
Rosh Hashanah: The Jewish New Year festival.

Sabbath: The day during the week when Jews do not do work of any kind.
Sacrament of the sick: A service in the Roman Catholic Church where holy oil is put on a sick or dying person.
Saint: A holy man or woman.
Salat: The Muslim word for prayer.
Salvation Army: The Christian Church well-known for its practical work to help people in need.
Saum: One of the Five Pillars of Islam, the one about fasting.
Scribe: A Jewish leader in the time of Jesus.
Scriptures: The holy books of any religion.
Seder: The meal held by Jews on the first night of the festival of Pesach.
Sermon: The part in a Christian service where someone, usually the priest, explains some part of the Bible.
Sewa: Acts of kindness carried out by Sikhs.
Shabbat: The Jewish holy day, also known as the Sabbath Day.
Shahadah: The Muslim belief in God.
Shalwar-Kameez: Tunic worn by Sikh brides.
Shema: The short statement which explains what a Jew believes about God.
Shiva: The first seven days of mourning after a Jewish person has died.

PUPILS' GLOSSARY

Shofar: A ram's horn blown during some Jewish festivals.
Siddur: The Jewish prayer book.
Sign of the cross: The outline of a cross marked on someone's forehead in church
Sikh: A man or a woman who follows the teachings of Sikhism.
Sikhism: The religion which follows the teachings of Guru Nanak.
Sunday: The day on which most Christians go to church.
Synagogue: A Jewish place of worship.

Tallit: The shawl worn by Jewish men when they pray.
Tefillin: Leather boxes worn by Jewish men and which contain the Shema.
Temple: The building in Jerusalem where Jews worshipped God; destroyed by the Romans in 70 C.E.
Ten Sayings: The most important Jewish laws believed to have been given by God to Moses on Mt Sinai.
Torah: The first five books of the Jewish Scriptures, known as the 'book of the law'.
Turban: Head-covering worn by all Sikh men.

Vatican: The home of the Pope in Rome
Vegetarian: Someone who does not eat any meat.
Vicar: The man or woman who looks after a church and conducts services in a Church of England or Church in Wales church.
Virgin Mary: The mother of Jesus.

Waheguru: The Sikh name for God.
Wesley, John: The founder of the Methodist Church.

Yad: A metal pointer used by Jews when reading from a scroll in a synagogue.
Yarmulka: Skull-cap worn by all Jewish men in the synagogue.
Yom Kippur: The holiest day in the Jewish year, also called the 'Day of Atonement'.

Zakat: The giving of money by Muslims to help the poor.

TEACHER'S GLOSSARY

TEACHER'S GLOSSARY

Abraham: The first Jew to believe in just one God, and the 'father' of the Jewish religion.
Adhan: The call to prayer made five times each day from the minaret of a mosque.
Adi Granth: The more condensed version of the sacred Scriptures of Sikhism; see also Guru Granth Sahib.
Adult baptism: Also known as 'Believer's Baptism', or baptism by immersion; the practice in the Baptist Church of only baptizing believing adults by fully immersing them in water.
Akhand Path: A non-stop, 48-hour reading of the Adi Granth, carried out on special occasions in Sikhism, e.g. following someone's death.
Allah: The name given to the supreme being worshipped by Muslims.
Altar: The holiest part of a Christian church. The place where Holy Communion or the Mass is celebrated.
Amrit: Sugared water used by Sikhs at infancy ceremonies and at the initiation into the Khalsa.
Amrit Pahul: The name given to the ceremony at which Sikhs are inaugurated into the Khalsa.
Anand Karaj: The 'ceremony of bliss', the Sikh wedding service.
Anglo-Catholic: A member of the Church of England who incorporates many religious practices taken from the Roman Catholic Church into his or her worship.
Aqiqah: The naming ceremony for Muslim babies.
Archbishop of Canterbury: The main priest in the Church of England and the leader of the Anglican communion worldwide.
Arranged marriages: The custom followed in both Islam and Sikhism whereby relations arrange the marriages of younger members of their families.

Baptism by immersion: See adult baptism.
Baptist Church: The Free Church which only baptises adults.
Barmitzvah: 'Son of the commandment', the ceremony in a Jewish synagogue to mark a boy's reaching of adulthood, i.e. on his 13th birthday.
Batmitzvah: 'Daughter of the commandment' a ceremony only held in Reform and Liberal synagogues to mark the age at which a girl reaches maturity, i.e. on her 12th birthday.
Bat Hayil: 'Daughter of Valour', a ceremony held in some Orthodox Jewish synagogues to mark a girl's 12th birthday.
Believer's baptism: See adult baptism.
Bible: The holy book of Christians, made up of the Old and New Testaments.
Bishop: Senior priests in the Roman Catholic Church or the Anglican Church.
Bismillah: Phrase meaning 'in the name of God, the merciful, the compassionate', used at beginning of every sura (chapter) in the Qur'an except one. Also the name given to the ceremony to mark a Muslim child's first lesson in the Qur'an.
Book of Common Prayer: The prayer book used in the Church of England since the 16th century, now superseded in many churches by the Alternative Service Book.
Brit Millah: The Jewish practice of circumcising boys at the age of eight days.

Cardinal: The most important priests in the Roman Catholic Church.
Chapel: A small church. The usual name for a Methodist place of worship
Chevra Kadisha: The Jewish group of volunteers who help as someone is dying and make all the funeral arrangements afterwards.
Chrismation: The anointing with oil which is part of infant baptism in the Orthodox Church.
Church of England: The Church formed by Henry VIII and the Established Church in England, part of the Anglican Communion.
Circumcision: The religious practice, called Brit Millah, which Jews carry out when a boy is eight days old. The foreskin of the penis is snipped leaving the glans permanently exposed.
Citadel: A Salvation Army place of worship.

TEACHER'S GLOSSARY

Confession: The Roman Catholic practice of confessing sins to a priest.
Confirmation: The service in the Church of England or the Roman Catholic Church in which a person 'confirms' the promises that others made for them when they were baptised.
Cremation: The burning of dead bodies. Sikhs will only cremate their dead. Often widely used by Christians now as well.

David: The second king of Israel; the most successful of all Israelite kings, defeating all of the nation's enemies. Known as Israel's most loved king.
Day of Atonement: 'Yom Kippur', the most solemn day in the Jewish calendar.
Denomination: A branch of the Christian Church.
Disciple: A description of a learner, or pupil of any religious leader, usually applied to the followers of Jesus and Buddha.
Divine Liturgy: The most important service in the Orthodox Church, the celebration of Holy Communion.
Diwan: The morning service of worship in a gurdwara consisting of prayers, hymns and readings from the Guru Granth Sahib.
Dowry: Sum of money paid by a groom to a bride on their marriage, to safeguard the bride against divorce or the death of her husband.
Du'a: Spontaneous prayer in Islam.

Evangelical: A Christian of any Protestant denomination who believes in personal conversion to Christ and the literal truth of the Bible.

Fast: Refraining from eating and, sometimes, drinking for a set period of time as a spiritual discipline.
Five Ks: The distinctive items of dress which characterise members of the Sikh Khalsa – kesh (uncut hair); kangha (comb); kirpan (sword); kachs (shorts) and kara (bracelet).
Font: A receptacle or container, often made of stone, found just inside the door of many Christian churches. Water to be used in infant baptism is kept in the font.
Free Church: Churches which are not members of the Church of England, Roman Catholic or Orthodox Churches, e.g. the Baptist and Methodist Churches.

Granthi: An official in the gurdwara, whose task is to look after the Guru Granth Sahib.
Gurdwara: A Sikh community centre used for worship and other gatherings. Contains a temple in which the Guru Granth Sahib is kept and a langar (an open kitchen).
Guru: A holy man or teacher in the Eastern religions. Particularly important in Sikhism where there were ten Gurus.
Guru Gobind Singh (1666-1708). The last of the ten Sikh Gurus. Taught the people that the title 'Guru' would from then on be conferred on the holy book.
Guru Granth Sahib: The holy book of the Sikh religion containing the Adi Granth and other writings.
Guru Nanak (1469-1539): The first Guru. Guru Nanak was the founder of Sikhism.

Hadith: Teachings and sayings about the life of Muhammad.
Heaven: In the Bible heaven is described as the place where God and his angels live. It is also the final destination of the righteous. In the Qur'an heaven is called 'paradise'.
Hebrew: The language in which the Jewish Scriptures are written and in which modern synagogue services are conducted.
Holy Communion: The term used for the central act of worship in the Church of England. It is the communion of the people with God through receiving the bread and wine.
Holy Spirit: The third person of the Christian Trinity (Godhead). The others are God the Father and God the Son. The Holy Spirit is usually represented by a dove.

TEACHER'S GLOSSARY

Huppah: The canopy standing on four legs underneath which a Jewish bride and groom stand during the wedding service. The huppah represents the home that the couple will set up together.

Icon: A religious painting of Jesus Christ, the Virgin Mary or one of the saints. Used particularly in the Orthodox Church as an aid to personal devotion and holiness.
Iconostasis: The screen in Orthodox churches, covered with icons, which separates the sanctuary from the nave. The congregation can just see the altar through the Royal Doors in the iconostasis.
Imam: The Muslim leader who directs public worship in the mosque and elsewhere. The imam is usually chosen from amongst the congregation.
Incense: Gum or spice which is burnt to produce a sweet smell. Used particularly in Roman Catholic, Orthodox and High Anglican services during worship.
Infant baptism: The practice of the Church of England, the Roman Catholic and Orthodox Churches of baptising babies.

Jerusalem: The holy city which is sacred to Christianity, Judaism and Islam. The city where Jesus was crucified and which contains the mosque known as the Dome of the Rock.
Jesus: The Jew, who Christians believe to be the Son of God, who founded the Christian religion.
Jew: A man or a woman who has a Jewish mother.
Jibril (Gabriel): The angel who visited Muhammad and brought him revelations from God, which form the basis of the Qur'an.
John the Baptist: The cousin of Jesus, the preacher who taught people to repent and be baptised in preparation for the coming of Jesus.

Kaaba: The Islamic shrine in Makkah which contains the Black Stone and is said to have been built by Ibrahim (Abraham) and his son, Ismail (Ishmael).
Kaddish: A Jewish prayer praising God, said by those who have recently lost a close relative.
Kangha: A comb which members of the Sikh Khalsa use to control their hair. One of the Five Ks.
Kara: A steel bracelet worn by members of the Khalsa. One of the Five Ks.
Karah Parshad: A mixture of flour, butter, sugar and water which is shared at the end of all Sikh services.
Kesh-Dhari: A Sikh who keeps some of the rules of the Khalsa, including having long hair, but who has not been baptised.
Ketubah: The marriage document given to a Jewish bride setting out the duties of the groom.
Khalsa: The Sikh brotherhood. Members promise to wear the Five Ks.
Kirpan: A sword worn by members of the Khalsa. One of the Five Ks.

Langar: The open kitchen attached to a gurdwara where the congregation have a meal together after worship.
Laying on of hands: The practice of a bishop laying his hands on the head of a worshipper to pass on a spiritual blessing.
Liturgy: An order of service which follows a prescribed pattern. The main Churches tend to have clearly defined liturgies; the Free Churches do not.

Madressa: The school in which Muslim children learn the Arabic language and the meaning of their religion.
Mahr: The gift given by a Muslim groom to his bride.
Makkah: The birthplace of the Prophet Muhammad and the most sacred city in Islam. The location of the Kaaba.
Marriage contract: The contract between a Muslim bride and groom which stipulates the size of the mahr.
Mass: The main service of the Roman Catholic Church during which Catholics believe the bread and wine turn into the body and blood of Jesus.

TEACHER'S GLOSSARY

Methodist Church: The Free Church formed in the eighteenth century by John Wesley.
Minister: The priest in a Free Church.
Mitzvot: The commandments which the Jewish Scriptures and tradition place on all Jewish people.
Mohel: A Jewish man trained to circumcise boys after eight days.
Moses: The Jewish leader who led Israel out of Egyptian slavery and instructed the people about God's laws.
Mosque: A Muslim place of worship.
Muhammad: The Prophet of Allah; founder of Islam.

Nonconformist: A member of a Free Church.

Onan: The name given to someone of the Jewish faith who is in mourning, between the times of the death and burial of their relative.
Ordination: The ritual by which a man or a woman is installed into the priesthood of the Church.
Orthodox Church: Originally the Church of the eastern part of the Roman Empire. The separation of the East (Orthodox) and West (Roman Catholic) came during the Great Schism of 1054.

Panj Pyares: Originally the first members of the Khalsa inaugurated by Guru Gobind Singh. Five experienced Sikhs represent them in the initiation ceremony into the Khalsa.
Patka: The small head-covering worn by Sikh boys before they are able to tie a turban for themselves.
Peter, Saint: One of the disciples of Jesus. Thought by Roman Catholics to have been the first Bishop of Rome and so the first Pope.
Polygamy: The practice of one man being able to take more than one wife.
Pope: The chief bishop of the Roman Catholic Church and the Bishop of Rome.
Priest: An official mediator between God and worshippers.
Protestant: A person who belongs to a church other than the Orthodox or Roman Catholic Churches.
Punjab: The area in North India which is the spiritual home of Sikhs.
Purgatory: In Catholic belief, the intermediate place between heaven and hell.

Qur'an: The holy book of Muslims. Believed to have been given by revelation through the Angel Jibril to Muhammad.

Rabbi: The title given to someone who is an authorised teacher in the Jewish faith.
Registry Office: The place authorised to conduct non-religious weddings.
Reincarnation: Belief of Sikhs and Buddhists that death is not the end and that the soul is reborn many times.
Roman Catholic Church: The worldwide community of Christians which owes allegiance to the Pope as the successor of St Peter.
Rosh Hashanah: The Jewish New Year recalling the work of God in creating the world.

Sacrament: An outward sign of an inward, spiritual blessing. In the Church of England there are two sacraments, and seven in the Roman Catholic and Orthodox Churches.
Sacrament of the sick: The anointing of the sick and dying by a Roman Catholic priest. One of the seven sacraments recognized by the Catholic Church.
Sahaj-Dhari: Sikhs who are seeking God, but who do not join the Khalsa.
Saint: A person of outstanding religious devotion which is recognised by the Church.
Salvation Army: The Protestant organization founded by William and Catherine Booth in 1880.
Scriptures: The holy writings of any religion.
Sefer Torah: The scrolls on which the Torah is written.
Sewa: An act of kindness in the Sikh faith.

TEACHER'S GLOSSARY

Shabbat: The holy day of Judaism running from sunset on Friday to Saturday evening.
Shalwar-Kameez: Tunic worn by Sikh brides at their wedding.
Shahadah: The first pillar of Islam which speaks of the greatness of Allah – and the fact that Muhammad is his Prophet.
Shiva: The first seven days of mourning after the death of someone in the Jewish faith.
Shofar: The ram's horn blown during Rosh Hashanah and other Jewish festivals.
Sign of the cross: The shape of a cross traced on the forehead of worshippers by a bishop during Confirmation, baptism and other services.
Sohilla: The final prayer of the day, recited before a Sikh goes to bed.
Soul: The 'spiritual' part of the human personality often considered to be immortal.
Synagogue: The building used for Jewish worship.

Tallit: Jewish prayer-shawl of white material with fringes in which there is a blue thread. Worn by Jewish men at all morning services.
Talmud: The most important source of Jewish law.
Tefillin: Two small boxes which are sometimes fastened to a Jewish man's head and left arm. They contain four passages from the Jewish Scriptures.
Temple: The Jewish place of worship in Jerusalem first erected by Solomon around 950 BCE.
Tenakh: Jewish term for their Scriptures.
Ten Commandments: See Ten Sayings.
Ten Sayings: The ten laws given by God to Moses on Mount Sinai. Christians called them the Ten Commandments.
Thirty-nine Articles: Statement of beliefs of the Church of England dating from the 16th century. Clergy must give their assent to them before they are ordained.
Torah: The books of the Law, i.e. the first five books of the Jewish (and Christian) Scriptures. They are Genesis, Exodus, Leviticus, Numbers and Deuteronomy.
Turban: Length of cloth wound around the head by Sikh men.

Ummah: The worldwide Muslim community.

Vatican: The residence of the Pope next to St Peter's Basilica in Rome.
Virgin Mary: Mother of Jesus Christ. Thought by Roman Catholics to have remained a virgin for all of her life.

Wesley, John (1703-1791): Initially an Anglican clergyman, he was 'converted' in 1738. Ordained own clergymen and built churches as he founded the Methodist Church.

Yad: Metal finger pointer used to follow the text in a scroll in synagogue.
Yarmulka: The skull-cap worn by Jewish men in the synagogue and elsewhere.
Yom Kippur: Most solemn day in Jewish year, the Day of Atonement, a day for fasting, repentance and prayer.

Junior Steps in RE

Year 5

This invaluable series offers all the support and resources necessary to teach RE successfully to 7 to 11 year olds.

- Covers all educational and legal requirements for teaching RE
- Covers Christianity plus Judaism, Islam and Sikhism
- Packed with background information
- Stimulating discussion material and practical starting points
- Photocopiable pages provide the teacher with extra resources
- Contains glossaries of specialist words and terms for both pupils and teachers

Available in this series for Years 3 to 6: *Junior Steps in RE Teacher's Book* and *Junior Steps in RE Pupils' Book*.

STANLEY THORNES

Ellenborough House
Wellington Street
CHELTENHAM
Glos. GL50 1YW

ISBN 0-7487-2123-1

9 780748 721238